D1398058

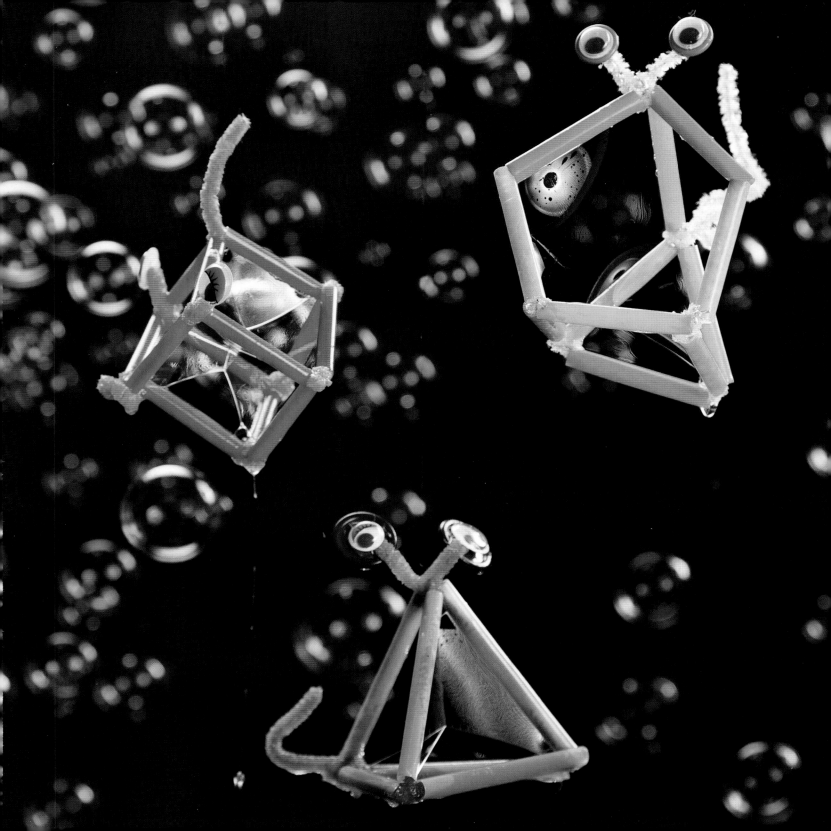

Brimming with creative inspiration, how-to projects, and useful information to enrich your everyday life, Quarto Knows is a favorite destination for those pursuing their interests and passions. Visit our site and dig deeper with our books into your area of interest: Quarto Creates, Quarto Cooks, Quarto Homes, Quarto Lives, Quarto Drives, Quarto Explores, Quarto Gifts, or Quarto Kids.

© 2019 Quarto Publishing Group USA Inc. Text © 2019 Sam Haynor

First published in 2019 by Young Voyageur Press, an imprint of The Quarto Group, 100 Cummings Center, Suite 265-D, Beverly, MA 01915, USA. T (978) 282-9590 F (978) 283-2742 QuartoKnows.com

Young Voyageur Press titles are also available at discount for retail, wholesale, promotional, and bulk purchase. For details, contact the Special Sales Manager by email at specialsales@quarto.com or by mail at The Quarto Group, Attn: Special Sales Manager, 100 Cummings Center, Suite 265-D, Beverly, MA 01915, USA.

10 9 8 7 6 5 4 3 2 1

ISBN: 978-0-7603-6445-1

Digital edition published in 2019
eISBN: 978-0-7603-6446-8

Library of Congress Cataloging-in-Publication Data

Names: Haynor, Sam, 1985- author.
Title: Curious creatable creatures : 22 STEAM projects that magnetize, glide, slingshot, and sometimes scootch / Sam Haynor.
Description: Minneapolis, Minnesota : Young Voyageur Press, 2019. | Audience: Ages 8-12.
Identifiers: LCCN 2018051034 | ISBN 9780760364451 (flexi-bound)
Subjects: LCSH: Toy making--Juvenile literature. | Mechanical toys--Juvenile literature. | Squeak toys--Juvenile literature. | Handicraft--Juvenile literature.
Classification: LCC TT174 .H3895 2019 | DDC 745.592 |2 23
LC record available at https://lccn.loc.gov/2018051034

Printed in China

Acquiring Editor:
Thom O'Hearn

Project Manager:
Alyssa Lochner and Alyssa Bluhm

Art Director:
Laura Drew

Cover & Page Designer:
Evelin Kasikov

Layout:
James Kegley

Photography:
Jeffery Schwinghammer
& Sam Haynor

Illustrations:
Trevor Spencer

Photo Stylist:
Young Xie

CURIOUS CREATABLE CREATURES

22
STEAM Projects That Magnetize, Glide, Slingshot, and Sometimes Scootch

Sam Haynor

young
voyageur

CONTENTS

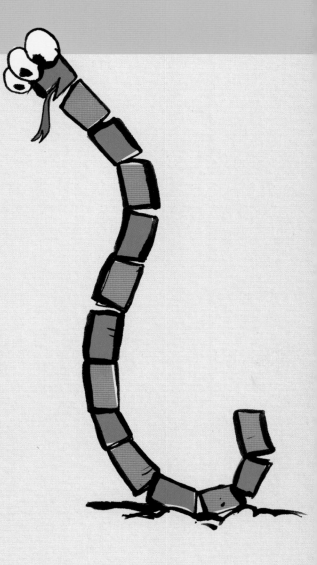

INTRODUCTION

OH, LOOK!
IT'S OUR FAVORITE HUMAN!

Hey, hey, Reddi! Look, it's a human! We've heard all the stories, like that you have five-fingered tentacles and twice as many eyes as a cyclops. Our friends are never going to believe you exist. But we're glad you're here!

Your timing couldn't be better: Reddi and I were just reading a book about creatures. Have you ever heard of the Windy Wheelums or Yarny Yip-Yaps? It's all very exciting, but now we want to see them up close. Let's go find some!

Ah, right. The thing with creatures and monsters is that they have to be created first. (It still weirds us out that humans are "born" and all.) Here in Creature Kingdom, we're all *made*. You know, like, put together with glue and stuff. We would create all these creatures ourselves, but, as you know, we're tiny. With small hands. Made of wire.

You'll help us make them, won't you, human friend? Yes? Fantastic! We better get you set up with tools and everything. You can even practice by making us! Just remember to make me, your old friend Yullo, just a little more awesome than Reddi, okay?

Okay, ready? Let's GO!

YOUR CREATURE WORKSHOP

Because you're about to go on an adventure, you're probably wondering what to pack. We bet you have burning questions like, "How many sandwiches should I bring?" and "Just how many humans *have* escaped from the Spitting Spurlock?" Great questions! And, well, as this is an adventure, we don't have *all* the answers. We'd say to start by packing some imagination and checking out these creature-making tools and supplies. And remember—use what's around! Many of these supplies can be swapped out for things you already have. Experimenting is part of creature creation.

CREATURE TOOLS

- **Hot glue gun (A).** Glue keeps everything together, like the magician's wand of creature-making. Just be careful of the heat and grab an adult to help.

- **Pliers (B).** They're the strong robot fingers we all wish we had. Use them to bend and snip wire.

- **Scissors (C).** They're not just for paper. Follow us and you'll be chopping all sorts of materials with scissors in no time.

- **Drill (D).** This is great for creature-making, but also requires more caution than any of the creatures in this book. An adult will help you out with this power tool.

- **Wire strippers (E).** A fun new tool used to make electric creatures.

- **Markers (F).** Add designs to all your creatures to make them your own.

- **Paintbrush (G).** Treat your creature to a new paint job.

CREATURE SUPPLIES

- **Wire (H).** Great for bending arms, legs, and everything else.

- **Tape (I).** Tape can be useful when glue won't do.

- **Foam and felt (J).** When your creatures need color, look no further.

- **Stretchy things (K).** Balloons and rubber bands make creatures bounce.

- **Fasteners (L).** Keep your creatures together with a handy fastener or three.

- **Pompoms and pipe cleaners (M).** Bright pipe cleaners and pompoms make creatures look good.

- **Craft sticks (N).** They're the wood boards of the creature world.

- **Googly eyes (O).** How else would your creature see what's around them?

- **Beads and buttons (P).** Hard items like beads and buttons can make for fun creature bodies and heads.

- **Cups and containers (Q).** Let's face it: some creatures need to be contained.

- **Found objects (R).** Anything can turn into a creature with some imagination.

- **Special objects (S).** Look at each project to see if there's anything special you need. Some creatures require a unique piece or two.

Safety Things

In addition to creature bites, there are a few other things that might hurt if you use them incorrectly. Be careful with tools like hot glue guns and always let your adult helper decide what to do for the projects with drills. Projects where you need to be a little extra careful will have this symbol ❗ next to them to give you a heads-up.

Hooking Up Electronics

Some creatures need electricity to come alive. With these creatures, you will be making circuits with a battery, wires, and some neat electronics parts. The electronics can sometimes be tricky, so take time to test things out. Aluminum foil wrapped around connections can help electricity flow, and hot glue or tape can help the wires stick together. Don't worry too much: the projects will all have helpful photos.

Keep Trying

Some steps can be hard at first, especially the ones marked "Tricky Step!" ◎ But don't give up, because getting those steps right might mean learning something new. If you feel yourself get really stuck, look at the photos again or ask a friend or adult for help. Two minds are better than one!

IT'S TIME TO DRILL!

Drills are great for making circular holes in things. But because they can be dangerous, your adult helper should decide whether they use the drill or whether you're ready to try. If you get to drill a hole, you'll want to know a couple things first. To make holes, you'll need *bits*, which are the long things that you screw into the end of drills. It's best to have a set with a couple of different sizes of bits. It's also great to have a surface that you can drill on that's okay to scratch up, because once you drill the hole you mean to drill, you don't want to accidentally drill a hole into your table. A scrap piece of wood works really well, and you can use it over and over again. When you drill, make sure to pay close attention. Use both hands but keep your fingers away from the drilling.

STEAM STUFF

As you make the creatures in this book, you'll see the word "STEAM" here and there. Now, you might be familiar with steam, which is what comes out of a teapot. But this is a different type of STEAM. It stands for: Science, Technology, Engineering, Art, and Math. Don't let those words scare you off. It's all about making stuff and figuring out how what we create relates to other things in the world. When you wire up the Electromagnetic Mooligan, make Honksee the Popstar sing, or send a Zippin' Zozot flying down the line, that's STEAM!

Experiment!

Not only can you customize the way the creatures look, but you can change how they act too! Experiment to see what changing some part of your creature does to the way it acts. Can your creature honk louder? Launch higher? Fly faster? After you make a creature, there's so much you can change to make it even more curious! Try out your ideas and see what works best.

LET'S GET MAKING!

MAKING REDDI AND YULLO

Before you flip through the book and make your favorite creature, why not make your fearless guides? That's us! You'll see us on many of the pages in this book, but we're even more fun in real life. If you've got a battery handy, we can light right up!

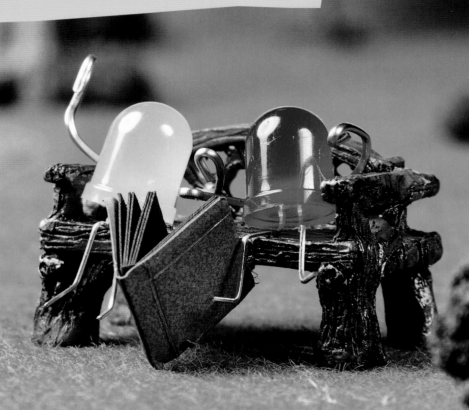

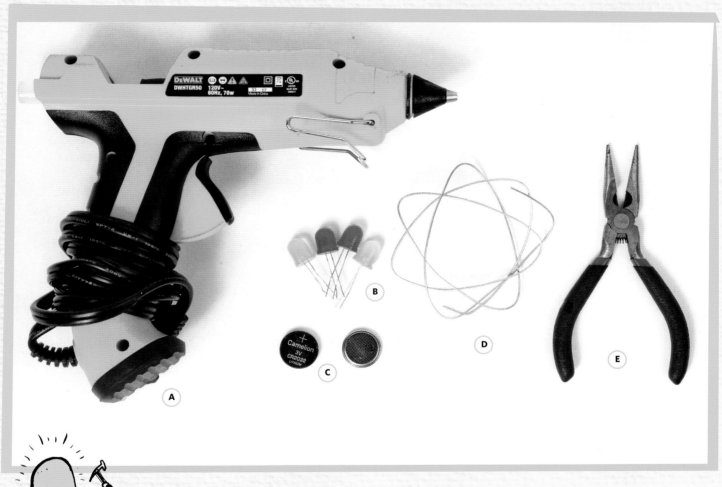

YOU WILL NEED

(A) Glue gun   (B) 2 big LEDs (1 yellow and 1 red)   (C) 3-volt button cell battery

(D) 12 inches thick steel wire   (E) Pliers

MAKE YOUR CREATURE

1. **CUT AND BEND LED LEGS.** Use pliers to cut the legs to the same length, and then bend them to make feet.

2. **BEND WIRE ARMS.** Cut a short piece of wire and curl both ends to make arms with hands.

3. **GLUE ARMS AROUND WAIST.** Bend arms around LED and dab with hot glue.

4. **LET IT GLOW.** Hold legs against both sides of your battery, and watch the LED light up! Flip the battery if the LED doesn't light up the first time.

5. **MAKE LOTS OF FRIENDS!** Reddi and Yullo come from a big family, after all. Make a whole crew!

STEAM STUFF
BRIGHT LIGHTS

Reddi and Yullo are kind, but a little light in the head. Or rather, they have a little light for a head. When you touch their legs to either side of the battery, you are completing a circuit that lights them up. The electric charge passes from 1 side of the battery, through 1 leg, through a connection in the head, through the other leg, and back through the battery. As the electricity passes through the head, it lights up! Where are there circuits in your everyday life?

EXPLORE SOME MORE

Reddi and Yullo are explorers. You can make tools for them to hold, scenes for them to be in, or even entire worlds. Try making a scene and photographing it from their perspective. What are some objects that are small to you that might be huge to Reddi and Yullo?

1

IMAJI NATIONAL PARK

PLEASE KEEP TENTACLES INSIDE THE VEHICLE AT ALL TIMES!

You are now entering Imaji National Park, home to creatures cuddly and carnivorous. On your tour, please do not feed any of the other guests to the creatures, and make sure to apply plenty of bite-spray. We will soon be passing through forested hills to witness the ancient **Long-Necked Gloveasaurus** (page 18), through the desert—watching out for **Scaly Slitheroons** (page 22), over boulder fields to see the mighty loogies of the **Spitting Spurlock** (page 26), and into the swamps in search of **Light-Up Crocodillies** (page 30).

And what's that over there? How did it get through the gates? Ummmm . . . run!

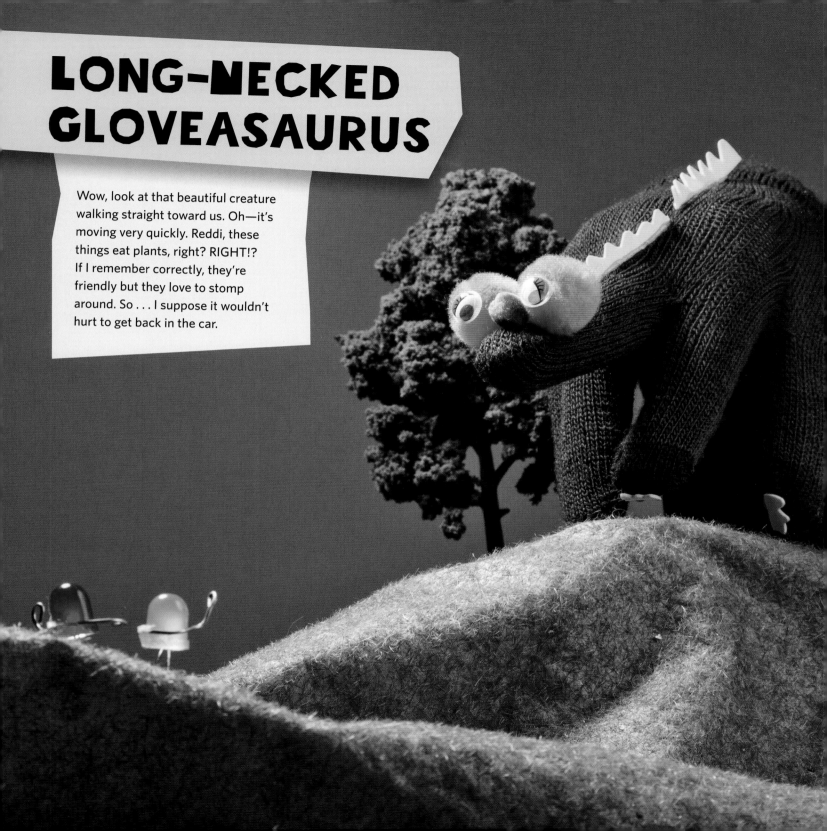

LONG-NECKED GLOVEASAURUS

Wow, look at that beautiful creature walking straight toward us. Oh—it's moving very quickly. Reddi, these things eat plants, right? RIGHT!? If I remember correctly, they're friendly but they love to stomp around. So . . . I suppose it wouldn't hurt to get back in the car.

FAST FACTS

WHAT: 4-legged plant-eating glove monster
STEAM STUFF: craft ▪ **DIFFICULTY:** ★ ▪ **COST:** $ $

YOU WILL NEED

Ⓐ Glue gun   Ⓑ Scraps of craft foam   Ⓒ 1 colorful glove   Ⓓ 2 googly eyes   Ⓔ A few pompoms   Ⓕ Scissors

I'M GLOVING IT! This project uses a glove, which can be a great craft item. Make sure you use a glove you have permission to craft with, so you don't annoy your family *too* much.

1. **STUFF A POMPOM INTO THE GLOVE'S MIDDLE FINGER.** This will give the dino's head some form.

2. **MAKE A FRIENDLY FACE.** Glue on pompoms and eyes to bring your Gloveasaurus to life. Is it scary or sweet or both?

3. **CUT AND GLUE FOAMY SCALES.** Glue foam along middle finger and then continue in a line up the wrist.

4. **CUT OUT 4 FOAM FEET.** Make them small enough to fit on the glove fingertips.

5. **GLUE FOAM FEET TO GLOVE FINGERTIPS.** Attach to the 4 non-face glove fingers.

6. **GO OUT FORAGING!** Take your Gloveasaurus out on a stroll. Eat trees! Dance on mountaintops! Celebrate being 65 million years young.

EXPLORE SOME MORE

No Gloveasaurus lives alone, so make a whole herd. Because gloves come in pairs, you have at least one other glove to try out another idea for what a Gloveasaurus can look like. Does it have pipe cleaner scales or big pompom feet? Maybe it has long eyelashes but big scary teeth. When you've made another Gloveasaurus, the best part is that you can still use your gloves to keep your hands warm. It's just that at any moment your hands can also turn into prehistoric beasts.

SCALY SLITHEROONS

Shhhhhhh . . . We have to walk very, very quietly through the sand dunes, or we might wake up the—AAAAAAH!!!! It's a Slitheroon! You know, they're not actually so scary after you get over the whole giant, terrifying snake thing. In fact, they can actually be pretty cute and they slither in fun ways. Awww, Reddi, can we keep this one?

FAST FACTS

WHAT: A segmented slithery creature that rides up and down a wire
STEAM STUFF: friction ▪ **DIFFICULTY:** ★ ▪ **COST:** $

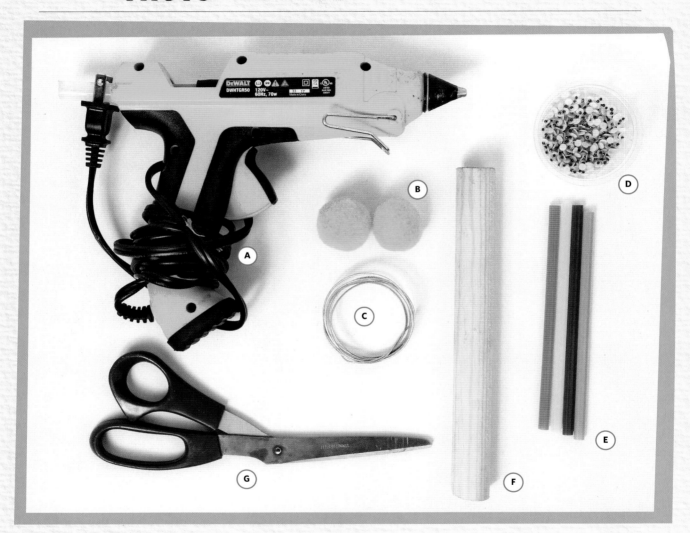

YOU WILL NEED

(A) Glue gun   (B) 2 pompoms   (C) 3 feet posable steel wire   (D) A few small googly eyes   (E) A few colorful straws

(F) 1 thick dowel (or other cylindrical object for wrapping wire around)   (G) Scissors

MAKE YOUR CREATURE

1. **COIL WIRE AROUND A THICK DOWEL.**

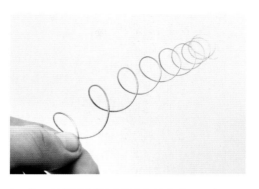

2. **SLIDE WIRE OFF DOWEL AND EXTEND.** Once the wire is off the dowel, pull the 2 wire ends to extend it. You can always adjust the wire later.

3. **GLUE A POMPOM ON ONE OF THE WIRE ENDS.** This will make a stopper to keep the Slitheroon's straw pieces on.

4. **CUT STRAWS INTO SIMILAR-SIZE SMALL PIECES.** They should look like small plastic loops.

5. **STRING ON STRAW LOOPS TO MAKE A SLITHEROON BODY.** String the loops onto the coiled wire. Make a neat color pattern!

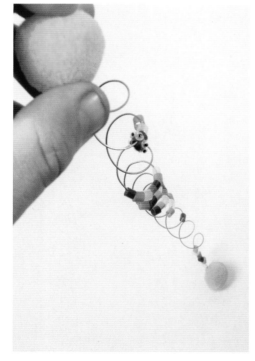

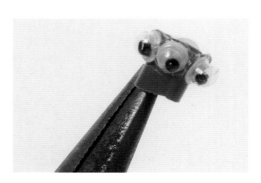

6. **MAKE A HEAD.** ◎ Glue tiny eyes or any other decorations you like onto your final straw piece.

7. **GLUE SECOND POMPOM ON OTHER WIRE END.** Now your Slitheroon shouldn't be able to slide off.

8. **TAKE YOUR SLITHEROON ON A WILD RIDE!** Flip the wire upside-down to send your Slitheroon slithering down the wire! When it's at 1 end, flip the wire again to make your Slitheroon come slithering back.

Try changing the shape of the wire that the Slitheroon rides down. You can pull, extend, bend, or compress the wire to see what a Slitheroon can do. You can also adjust the size of your straw loops to see what happens, or change your wire length to make a giant Slitheroon. How do you make a Slitheroon slither the fastest?

THE SPITTING SPURLOCK

Whoa! We've never been this close to a Spurlock! They'll just start spitting at the push of a button. Pretty bad manners, if you ask me. But, hey, no creature's perfect. Let's sneak up some more. Hmmm, do you think it's noticed us?

YOU WILL NEED

(A) Glue gun   (B) Ball of yarn   (C) 2 buttons   (D) Googly eyes   (E) 2 wooden beads   (F) 2 feet plastic tubing that fits tips of syringes   (G) 2 syringes (no needles)   (H) Scissors   (I) A few pompoms   (J) 1 can party string   (K) 8 pipe cleaners   (L) 2 wide craft sticks

WATCH WHERE YOU SPIT: Not everyone wants to play tag with a can of party string.

Make sure you are in a place where you can get stringy!

MAKE YOUR CREATURE

1. GLUE BEADS NEAR ENDS OF CRAFT STICKS.

2. MEASURE WHERE TO GLUE CRAFT STICKS ON CAN. Your syringe will be positioned with its 2 wings resting on the beads at the ends of the craft sticks. You want your syringe just above but not touching the button of the party string can when the plunger is pushed in.

3. GLUE CRAFT STICKS AND SYRINGE IN POSITION. Glue craft sticks to the sides of the can and the syringe's wings to the tops of the beads. Make sure the syringe's plunger end is near the can's button.

4. TEST THE SPIT BUTTON! ◉ Connect your hydraulic system by attaching 1 end of the tubing to the tip of the syringe. Then attach the other end of the tubing to the tip of the other syringe. Push the plunger of the second syringe. Play around with this attachment until you can make the plunger of the first syringe push the button on the can of party string.

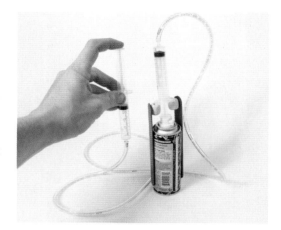

5. GIVE YOUR SPURLOCK A YARN SWEATER. Wrap the sides of the can so your Spurlock's body is warm and cozy. Finish with a dab of hot glue.

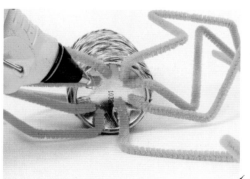

6. FOLD AND GLUE PIPE CLEANER LEGS TO BOTTOM OF CAN.

7. ADD SOME CHARACTER. Use pompoms, pipe cleaners, and googly eyes to give your Spurlock its charming face.

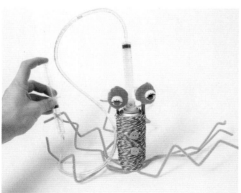

8. HAWK A LOOGIE! Push down on the second syringe and watch the party string fly!

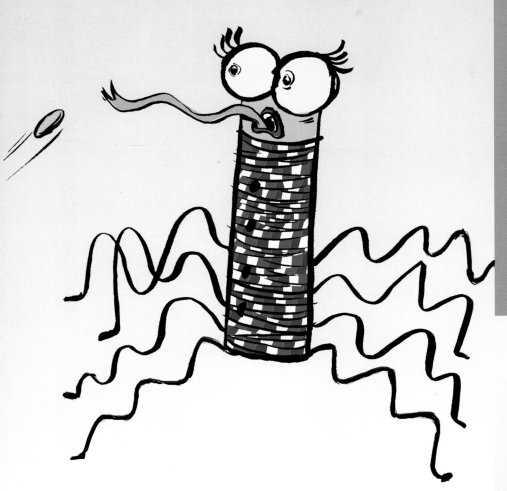

STEAM STUFF
PUSHING BUTTONS

Your Spitting Spurlock is a great example of a button pusher. In fact, you just made a *remote control* machine that doesn't need batteries. And now that you've designed one, where else could you use this in your life? Could you use the same system to turn off your lights from bed? Or turn off your alarm clock from across the room?

TRY IT!

If you need more force to make your Spurlock spit, try filling the second syringe and the tubing with water. That way when you push the plunger of the second syringe, the other plunger will press down much more forcefully. Why do you think water works better than air?

LIGHT-UP CROCODILLIES

Look at this loveable big-mouthed bunch coming our way! It's nice to see an entire family of Crocodillies together, especially when their lights are glowing. They will come right up to you, but the park rangers asked us not to feed them. Hey, Reddi—have you seen our dog?

FAST FACTS

WHAT: Clothespin chompers that light up with LEDs when their mouths are open
STEAM STUFF: electrical switches ▪ **DIFFICULTY:** ★ ★ ★ ▪ **COST:** $ $

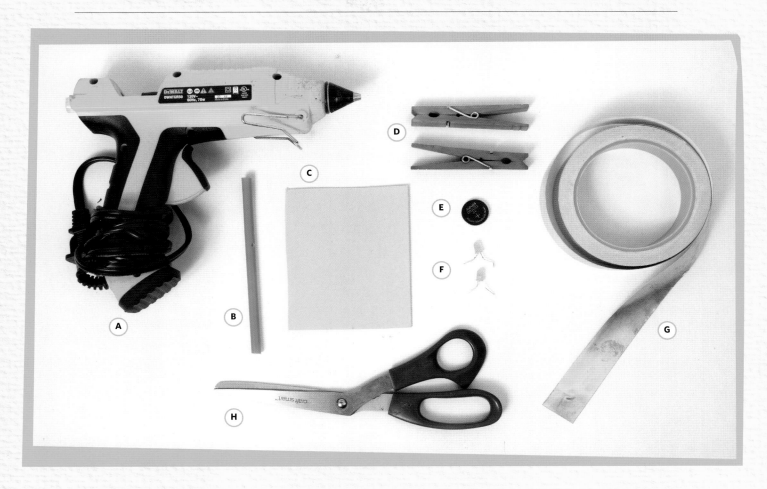

YOU WILL NEED

Ⓐ Glue gun Ⓑ 1 straw Ⓒ Scraps of craft foam Ⓓ 2 large clothespins Ⓔ 1 3-volt button cell (flat) battery

Ⓕ 2 LEDs Ⓖ Roll of copper tape Ⓗ Scissors

MAKE YOUR CREATURE

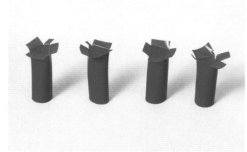

1. **GLUE CLOTHESPINS SIDE BY SIDE.** Line up the clothespins add a line of glue, making sure they can still open and close together.

2. **CUT AND GLUE FOAM SCALES.** Make 2 rows of triangles and glue them on top of the clothespins.

3. **MAKE STUMPY STRAW LEGS.** Cut small straw pieces and snip straw flaps at 1 end of each piece for easy gluing on the underside of the body.

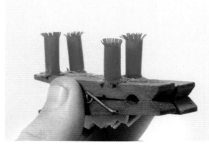

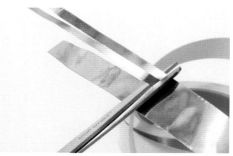

4. **GLUE LEGS ON AND MAKE FEET.** After you glue your legs onto the body, make a bunch of vertical snips at the foot end of each leg. Splay out the flaps to make some cute toes.

5. **FIT LEDS ON SCALES IN BACK.** Lay the LEDs across the scales so that the long legs of the LEDs are both on 1 side of the scales, and the short legs are on the other side.

6. **CUT THIN STRIPS OF COPPER TAPE.** Make each strip about 6 inches long and less than a quarter inch wide. We'll use these like wires for our electrical circuit.

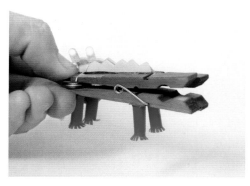

7. **RIGHT SIDE OF CREATURE: TAPE OVER LED LEGS AND TO THE INNER CLOTHESPIN CEILING.** ◎ Use 1 strip of copper tape to cover the right legs of the LEDs, leaving a few inches of tape off the back of the clothespin. Tuck the copper tape against the underside of the same arm of the clothespin, smoothing out any wrinkles.

8. **LEFT SIDE OF CREATURE: TAPE OVER LED LEGS AND TO THE INNER CLOTHESPIN FLOOR.** ◎ Use the other piece of copper tape to cover the left legs of the LEDs. Leave a little copper tape loose, and tape the rest to the top of the other wood arm of the clothespin.

9. **CHOMP TIME!** Place the battery in and squeeze! If the lights don't turn on, flip the battery over. Then go for the big chomp again!

STEAM STUFF
Which Switches?

When your Crocodillie opens its mouth, it acts like a light switch. When you squeeze the back, the battery and the LEDs connect, and your Crocodillie lights up. When you release the clothespins, the circuit is disconnected and the lights turn off. You just made an *electrical switch*! Electrical switches can come in so many forms. They can be buttons, volume knobs, dimmers, and anything else that turns things on and off. With copper tape, you can make a bunch of different kinds of switches to connect a battery to an LED circuit. What types can you think up and make?

TRY IT!

Your Crocodillie lights up when it opens its mouth. Can you make another circuit so the Crocodillie lights up when it closes its mouth? How would you design it?

2

CURIO CITY

WELCOME TO THE CITY THAT NEVER CREEPS!

We've got it all here in Curio City! **The Yarny Yip-Yaps** (page 36) will string you along, the **Windy Wheelums** (page 42) will blow you away, the **Electromagnetic Mooligans** (page 46) are a star attraction, and the **Watery Pumpitups** (page 50) will keep you feeling cool. It's Curio City: the city that never creeps. (Sometimes the Yip-Yaps do that thing where they pretend to be a haunted bowl of spaghetti, but it's not too creepy.) Let's go out on the town!

YARNY YIP-YAPS

Oh, look at all that fabulous hair! You should see these Yip-Yaps on a windy day. It's like a shampoo commercial on every block of Curio City. Remember when we had hair like that, Reddi? Just kidding. We've been bald as bowling balls since the day we were made.

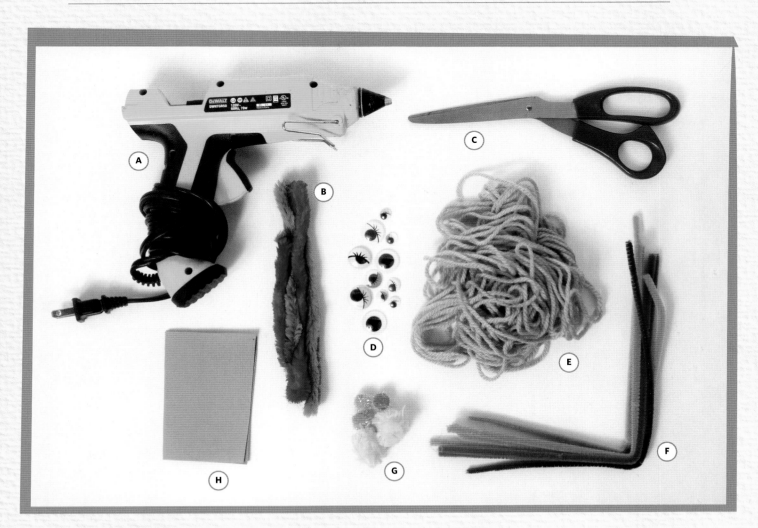

YOU WILL NEED

A Glue gun   B 2 pipe cleaners   C Scissors   D 2 googly eyes   E 1 ball colorful yarn   F Extra pipe cleaners (optional)

G A few pompoms   H Scraps of craft foam (optional)

MAKE YOUR MONSTER

1. **WRAP 4 FINGERS IN YARN.** Make 15 or more loops so your monster has plenty of hair.

2. **SLIDE A FOLDED PIPE CLEANER AROUND YARN.** Make sure 1 leg of the bent pipe cleaner goes on the inside of the yarn loop and the other is on the outside.

3. **TWIST PIPE CLEANER ON BOTH SIDES OF LOOPED YARN.** Twist the ends of the pipe cleaner to make what will be antennae, and twist the folded side to make a loop that will be the body. The yarn will be secure between the pipe cleaner twists.

4. **SLIDE YARN OFF YOUR HAND AND CUT.**
   ◎ Cut all the pieces of yarn on the opposite side of the loops from where the pipe cleaner is twisted. The loops will unfold to become the Yip-Yap's hair.

5. **STYLE YOUR HAIR.** Fold the body loop and style your Yip-Yap's hair around it. Don't fuss too much, as Yip-Yaps just don't have good hair days.

6. **ADD ANTENNAE EYES.** Glue pompoms and googly eyes to the 2 pipe cleaner ends.

7. **ADD A SECOND PIPE CLEANER TO MAKE ARMS.** Twist another pipe cleaner around the body twist. Stretch the ends out as arms. And then strike a pose!

8. **MAKE A YIP-YAP CREW!** Yip-Yaps love to live in bunches. Make a whole family of these colorful moplike beasts.

EXPLORE SOME MORE

Like snowflakes, no two Yip-Yaps are alike. Try wrapping yarn around something other than your hand before cutting, or try using multiple pipe cleaners to make a body and eyes. Add some craft foam moustaches, hats, and anything else to make your Yip-Yap family.

WINDY WHEELUMS

On your marks. Get set. Blow! If you've ever wanted to ride the wind, just grab on and don't let go. Wheelums will zoom city streets like racecars and spin around bends like tornados. Are you ready to get behind the wheel?

FAST FACTS

WHAT: Wind-powered cars that ride on poker chip wheels ▪ **STEAM STUFF:** air pressure ▪ **YOUR BIGGEST FAN:** This project uses the wind, and fans are the perfect engine. If you have a portable fan somewhere in your home, use it to get those Wheelums zooming. ▪ **DRILL TIME:** You'll need an adult helper with a drill to make your Windy Wheelums. See page 10 for more on drilling. ▪ **DIFFICULTY:** ★ ★ ▪ **COST:** $

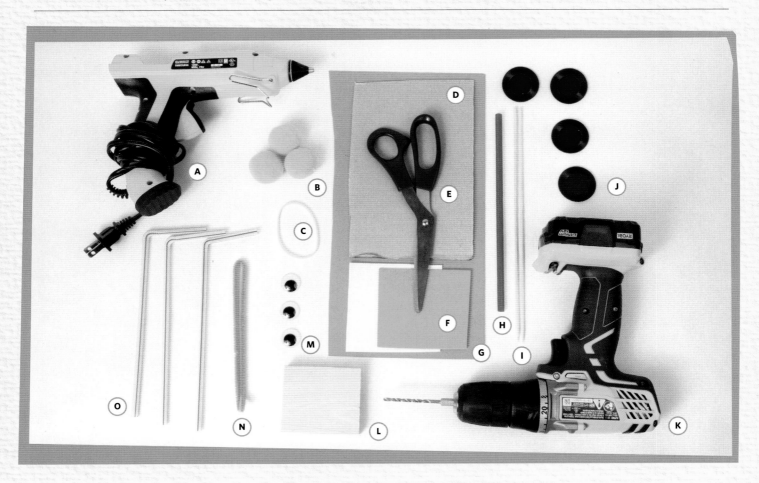

YOU WILL NEED

Ⓐ Glue gun   Ⓑ Pompoms   Ⓒ Rubber binder   Ⓓ 1 piece cardboard   Ⓔ Scissors   Ⓕ Scraps of craft foam

Ⓖ Large sheet craft foam   Ⓗ 1 straight straw   Ⓘ 2 thin wood skewers   Ⓙ 4 plastic poker chips (or other wheel substitute)

Ⓚ Drill, with small bit (size of wood skewer)   Ⓛ Wood block for drilling   Ⓜ Googly eyes   Ⓝ Pipe cleaner

Ⓞ Bendy straws   ● Fan (optional)

MAKE YOUR CREATURE

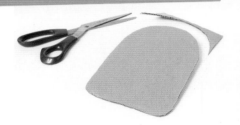

1. CUT A CARDBOARD BASE. Choose any shape you want, but make it at least 5 inches wide.

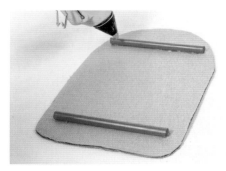

2. GLUE 2 STRAW PIECES TO BASE. Cut straw in half. Glue the 2 straw pieces parallel to each other on the base, with 1 piece at one end and the other piece at the other end.

3. DRILL HOLE IN CENTER OF 4 POKER CHIPS. ◎ Go slow and be careful, and make sure you have an adult's permission to drill. Make sure the holes are about the size of the wood skewers you're going to poke through them.

4. CUT WOOD SKEWER AXLES. Trim each axle so it is a little wider than your cardboard.

5. GLUE WHEELS ON AXLES. Use a dab of hot glue to secure your poker chips on the ends of the skewers.

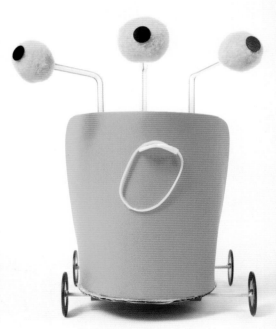

6. CUT AND GLUE FOAM SAIL. Make any shape of sail, and glue the base of the foam on 1 end of the cardboard base. A good design to start with is to make a large sail that wraps around the front of your Wheelum.

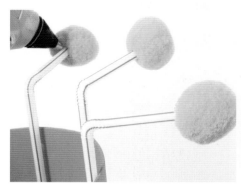

7. ADD SOME PERSONALITY! Every Wheelum needs a face. Add some eyes, some straw antennae, and a mouth to make your Wheelum monstrous.

8. *VROOM! VROOM!* RACE THAT WHEELUM! Use a fan or just use your breath. See how far your Wheelum can glide!

STEAM STUFF
AIR POWER

What gives your Wheelum its *vroom*? Your Wheelum is powered the same way a sailboat is. The sails on a ship are made to create a pocket that can capture wind. Every time a tiny bit of air hits the sail, it gives the ship a little nudge, which makes the ship go in that direction. When you have *lots* of air hitting the sail, you can build up a lot of speed. Experiment with your sail's shape to see what makes your Wheelum go faster.

EXPLORE SOME MORE

Your Wheelum needs something to race against! Make another Wheelum, and try out different designs. What happens if you change out the wheels or change the shape of the sail? What about adding more weight in the front or in the back? Does the Wheelum travel better backward or forward?

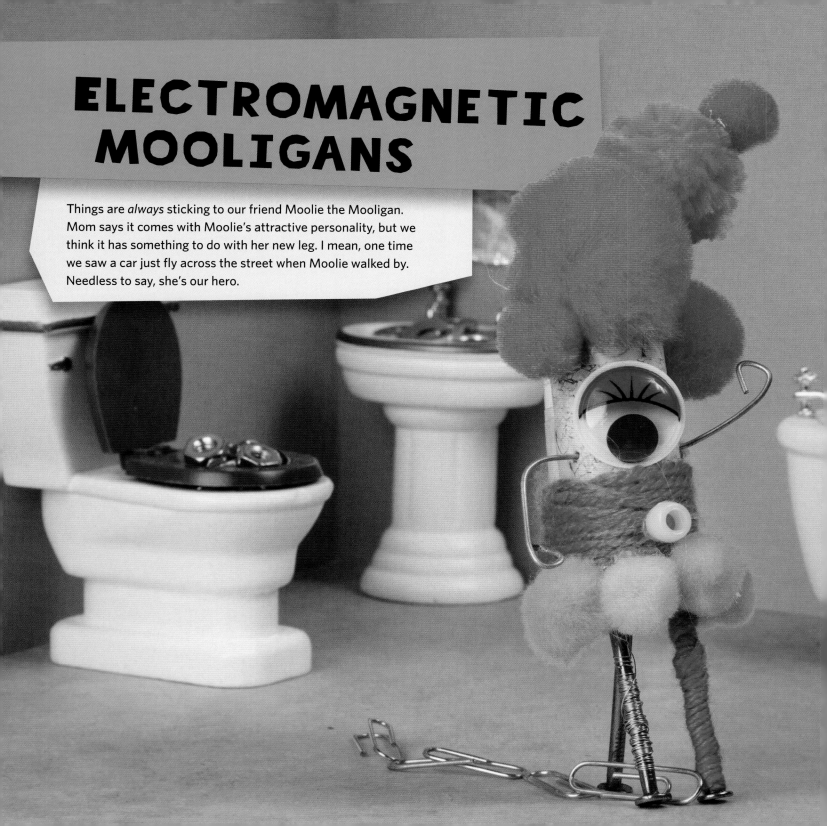

ELECTROMAGNETIC MOOLIGANS

Things are *always* sticking to our friend Moolie the Mooligan. Mom says it comes with Moolie's attractive personality, but we think it has something to do with her new leg. I mean, one time we saw a car just fly across the street when Moolie walked by. Needless to say, she's our hero.

FAST FACTS

WHAT: A creature that uses electricity to turn its legs into temporary magnets
STEAM STUFF: electromagnetism ■ **DIFFICULTY:** ★★★ ■ **COST:** $ $

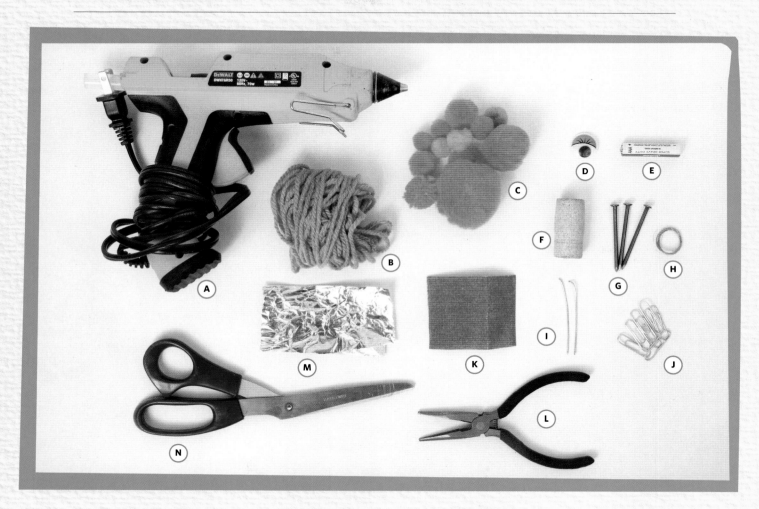

YOU WILL NEED

(A) Glue gun   (B) Some yarn   (C) Pompoms   (D) Googly eyes   (E) 1 AAA battery   (F) 1 cork   (G) 3 nails

(H) 3 feet of magnet wire   (I) 6 inches posable steel wire   (J) A few paper clips   (K) Sandpaper   (L) Pliers

(M) Scrap of aluminum foil   (N) Scissors   ● Masking tape

MAKE YOUR CREATURE

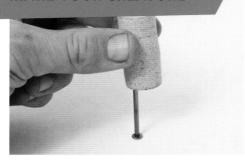

1. **PUSH A NAIL INTO THE BOTTOM OF THE CORK.**

2. **WRAP OR TAPE THE BATTERY TO THE CORK'S SIDE.** Use yarn or tape to make your Mooligan a battery backpack.

3. **SAND THE ENDS OF THE MAGNET WIRE.** Use the sandpaper to sand just 2 inches on each end of the magnet wire. The wire coating should disappear, revealing a brighter silver color underneath.

4. **SANDWICH ALUMINUM FOIL ON THE WIRE ENDS.** Make 2 small wads of aluminum foil surrounding both of the sanded wire ends.

5. **TAPE 1 FOIL-SANDWICHED END OF THE WIRE TO 1 END OF THE BATTERY.**

6. **WRAP THE NAIL IN MAGNET WIRE.** ◎ Wrap the other end of the magnet wire in tight loops around the nail until you have only a little wire left. Leave that hanging free with the aluminum foil on the end.

7. **TEST YOUR ELECTROMAGNET!** Hold the free end of the wire to the other end of the battery, and try to pick up some paper clips with the head of the nail. Does it work?

8. **ADD LEGS AND ARMS.** Push in 2 more nails for legs—now your Mooligan has 3 legs—and use pliers and steel wire to make posable metal arms.

9. **MAKE YOUR MOOLIGAN MARVELOUS.** Time to decorate! Add pompoms and googly eyes to make a fabulous wig and face.

10. STICK TO IT! Unleash the Mooligan's attractive power! See what metal objects it can pick up!

STEAM STUFF
ATTRACTIVE ELECTRICITY

Attraction can be fleeting. When you hold the foiled wire end to the battery, your *electromagnet* comes to life. You can suddenly pick up paper clips with your nail! The moment you stop pressing the foil end to the battery, the paper clips fall away. What's happening? You've created a temporary magnet. While some magnets are permanent (like those on a fridge), this one is only temporary. It works by electricity. When electricity goes through the many loops of wire around the nail, it turns the nail into a temporary magnet. This technology is used in almost all moving electric machines. If you find a machine that moves on its own and uses power, you can be sure there's an electromagnet somewhere inside. Can you find it?

EXPLORE SOME MORE

Test your power! If you want to make a stronger electromagnet, experiment by making more Mooligans. Try using a longer wire with more coils around the nail. Or maybe use a different kind of battery or battery pack. While you're experimenting, find out which metals your Mooligan can pick up and which ones don't budge. If you have some test objects, try sorting them into "sticks to Mooligan" and "doesn't stick to Mooligan" categories. Can you spot a pattern?

WATERY PUMPITUPS

Got a fire? Call the Pumpitups. Water slide running a little dry? Call the Pumpitups. Want a creature to talk with? You should probably call somebody else. Pumpitups don't really talk much. Their mouths are constantly full of water, and they mostly just spit. But they've saved Curio City more times than we count on our wire fingers, so they're good to have around.

WHAT: A life-saving, water-spitting beast   ■   **STEAM STUFF:** hydraulics and buttons
DIFFICULTY: ★ ★ ★   ■   **COST:** $ $

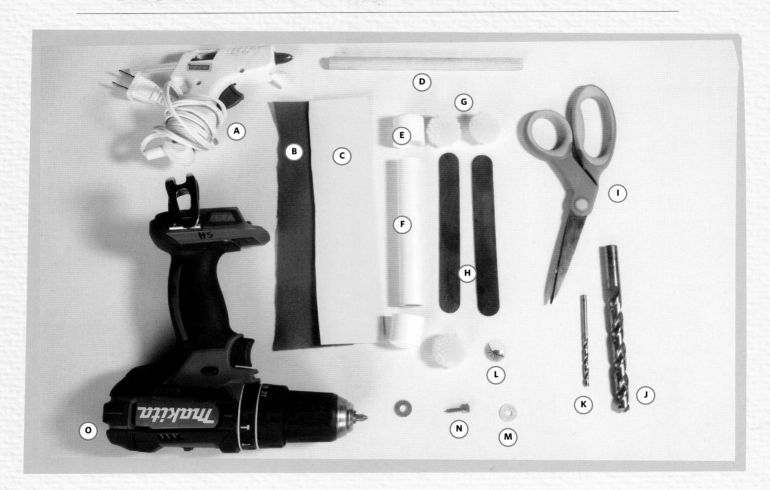

YOU WILL NEED

Ⓐ Glue gun   Ⓑ Felt   Ⓒ Medium-sized sheet of craft foam   Ⓓ Wood dowel (6 to 10 inches long)   Ⓔ 2 PVC caps (¾")
Ⓕ ¾" PVC pipe (6 to 10 inches long)   Ⓖ Pompoms   Ⓗ 2 craft sticks   Ⓘ Scissors   Ⓛ Googly eyes   Ⓜ 2 washers (½"
or sized to fit inside the PVC pipe)   Ⓝ 1 short wood screw   Ⓞ/Ⓙ/Ⓚ Drill, with large (width of dowel) and small drill bits,
and an adult helper to use it

1. **PRESS ONE END OF PVC PIPE INTO FOAM.** It should make a circular dent, which will be a guide for where to cut.

2. **CUT FOAM CIRCLE AND PUT BETWEEN 2 WASHERS ON A SCREW.** Cut just inside the indented circle on the foam. You can always trim this down later if it doesn't fit in the tube. Make a foam sandwich between the 2 washers.

3. **SCREW INTO END OF DOWEL.** Use a drill to screw the washers and foam firmly into the dowel. We'll call this the plunger.

4. **DRILL A HOLE IN EACH PVC CAP, 1 LARGE AND 1 SMALL.** ◎ The big hole should be big enough for the dowel to fit through. The caps are hard to hold on to, so have an adult help safely hold the cap in place with pliers or a wrench while drilling.

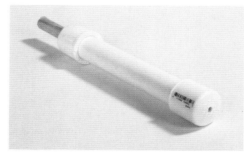

5. **PUT PLUNGER AND CAPS ON PVC TUBE.** Put the plunger into the tube, then press the caps on either end. The end of the plunger should fit through the cap with the big hole.

6. **ADD BODY DECORATION WITH A GLUE GUN.** Use felt and leftover foam to add your own style to your Pumpitup. A Pumpitup may not speak much, but it's still got flair.

7. **CUT AND ATTACH CRAFT STICK LEGS.** Use the rounded ends of the sticks to make 4 short legs to glue on.

8. **MAKE A SILLY FACE.** Combine pompoms, googly eyes, and anything else to give your Pumpitup a personality.

9. **PUMP IT UP!** Place its mouth in water, pull back the plunger to suck some up, and pump the plunger to let it fly! How far away could your Pumpitup be and still fight fires in Curio City? If it's not working, try adjusting or cutting a new foam circle for the plunger.

STEAM STUFF
LIFTING WATER

It's not so easy to make water go uphill. Imagine you had a river below your home. How could you bring water up to your kitchen? You might grab a bucket and move it up the hill a little at a time. Maybe you could move your home. You probably can't move the river. Perhaps the easiest way is to use a pump. Just look at the way your Pumpitup drinks water. When its mouth is underwater, and you pull back on its tail, water shoots up into the tube. You raise its mouth, and with a bop on its tail, it can spit the water right back out again. This is the basic way a pump works. Water at the bottom of a well? Use a pump to bring it up. Need to get water to a house at the top of the hill? A tube and a pump could save you many trips to the river. Where do you think there are pumps in your everyday life?

TRY IT!

A single Pumpitup can wear many mouths. If you have extra endcaps, try drilling different hole patterns in each. Can you make a pump that fires in a couple directions at the same time?

3

THE BEAST BAND IN TOWN

ARE YOU READY TO ROCK?

We've got a show tonight. And you have to come, because we're the best band around! Actually, we're more like the *BEAST* band around. Let's introduce you to the band. We've got the legendary **Trumpeting Trollygag** (page 56) who plays everything, the **HearMe Talkyou** (page 60) on backup vocals, and the otherworldly **Itty-Bitty Squeakadoos** (page 64) playing who-knows-what—plus, we're trying to convince **Honksee the Popstar** (page 70) to honk lead vocals tonight. We better make you an instrument too. Let's jam!

TRUMPETING TROLLYGAG

I know what you're thinking. How could we, Reddi and Yullo, convince the legendary Trumpeting Trollygag to play with us? Reddi, do you remember when Trolly was playing with Five-eyed Shoobs *and* the Great Tentacle? Too cool. Trolly plays the piano, the violin, and best of all, its trunk. When it starts to blow, wow! You'll just have to hear it for yourself.

FAST FACTS

WHAT: A loud trumpet played by blowing into its trunk
STEAM STUFF: vibration, sound ▪ **DIFFICULTY:** ★ ▪ **COST:** $

YOU WILL NEED

(A) Glue gun   (B) Pompoms   (C) Googly eyes   (D) Feathers   (E) Scissors   (F) 1 straw   (G) 1 pipe cleaner

(H) 1 cardboard tube   (I) 2 or 3 balloons   ● 1 rubber band

MAKE YOUR CREATURE

1. **CUT SLICE OUT OF A BALLOON.** It can be a very thin slice.

2. **STRETCH BALLOON OVER END OF TUBE AND SECURE WITH RUBBER BAND.** Use the new hole you cut, not the neck of the balloon, and pull over until the balloon is tight.

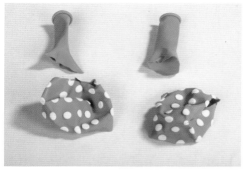

3. **CUT NECKS AND TOPS OFF OTHER 2 BALLOONS.** Make balloon bands with no top or bottom for Trolly's clothes.

4. **DRESS YOUR TROLLYGAG IN BALLOONS.** Stretch the bands over the cardboard tube to give Trolly an outfit.

5. **CUT OUT STRAW FEET.** Make small snips in the straw feet to splay out toes.

6. **GLUE FEET TO BOTTOM OF TUBE.** Add a dab of hot glue to secure each foot to the cardboard tube's rim.

7. **GLUE ON PIPE CLEANER ARMS.**

8. **GIVE YOUR TROLLYGAG A FACE.** Use pompoms, googly eyes, and feathers, but avoid gluing anything on the tight balloon surface on top.

9. **PLAY THAT FUNKY MUSIC!** Blow into the Trollygag's trunk to make it honk. Adjust the length of the tube or add on another to change the sound.

STEAM STUFF
WHERE'S THE WIGGLE?

When you play your Trumpeting Trollygag, something's wiggling. Can you figure out what it is? That wiggling, or *vibration*, is what moves the air back and forth and hits our ears as sound. Every instrument has something that wiggles back and forth to make the sounds we hear. Next time you see an instrument, see if you can find where.

TRY IT!

It takes some practice, but once you learn how to play a Trumpeting Trollygag, you never forget. Try making another with a longer cardboard tube and see how that changes its sound. Play on!

THE HEARME TALKYOU

They say the Hearme Talkyou twins are the best back-up singers in all of Creature Kingdom. (We say back-up singers because, with how loud they are, we usually back up.) They do sing well together, but if you try talking to one, you'll find the other just starts talking right away. Go on, give it a try.

WHAT: A two-way set of talking funnels ▪ **STEAM STUFF:** sound waves
DIFFICULTY: ★ ▪ **COST:** $ $

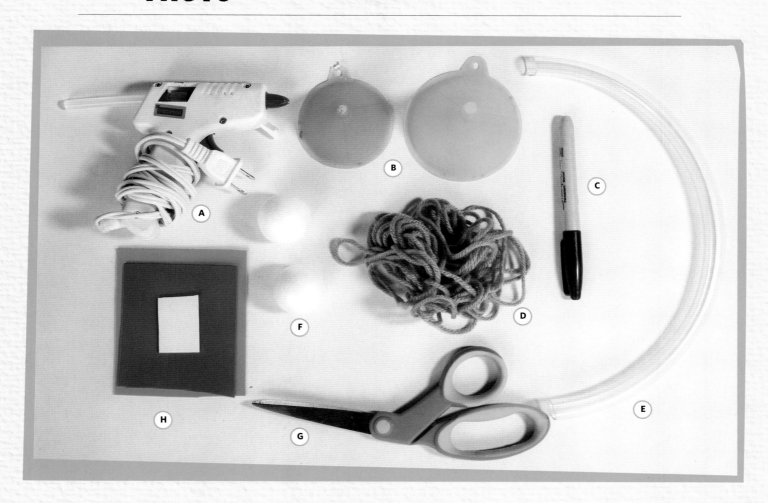

YOU WILL NEED

Ⓐ Glue gun   Ⓑ 2 funnels   Ⓒ Marker   Ⓓ Ball of yarn   Ⓔ Plastic Tubing (2 to 6 feet)   Ⓕ 2 Styrofoam balls

Ⓖ Scissors   Ⓗ 3 colors of craft foam (4-by-4-inch pieces)

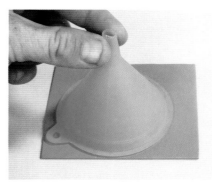

1. WRAP TUBE IN YARN.

2. GLUE YARN ENDS TO TUBE. A little dot of hot glue on both ends will do.

3. PRESS FUNNELS INTO FOAM. This indent will show you where to cut to make the foam lips.

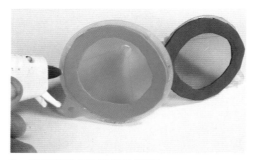

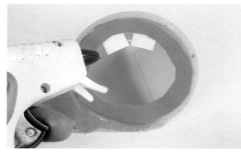

4. CUT OUT FOAM RINGS TO MAKE LIPS.

5. GLUE LIPS ON FUNNEL RIMS.

6. ADD TEETH. Cut out a few foam teeth and glue them to the backside of the lips.

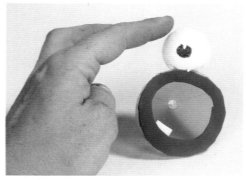

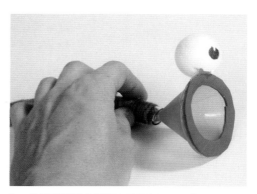

7. DRAW ON EYES. Use a marker to fill in those Styrofoam eyeballs.

8. PRESS OR GLUE EYES ON TO FUNNELS. You may need to cut a little notch in your eyeball for it to fit on the rim of the funnel before gluing.

9. GLUE FUNNELS INTO TUBE. Insert a funnel to each side of the tube and secure with a bit of glue.

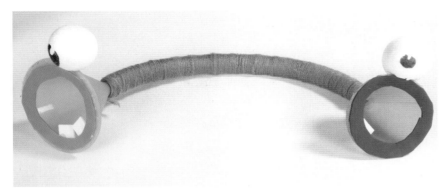

10. GIVE SOMEONE (OR YOURSELF) A CALL! You've got a call on Line 1. Talk into one end of your creature, and your voice comes out the other. How softly can you whisper and still hear out the other side?

STEAM STUFF
CHEAP TELEPHONES

Your voice likes to spread out. When you shout in a room, people can hear you no matter where in the room they are. But when you speak into a telephone, or even two cans on a string, your voice takes a narrow path. In the Hearme Talkyou, sound goes into one funnel, through the tube, and out the other—so if your tube is long enough, you can whisper to somebody standing in another room. How does it go through? When you speak, you wiggle the air back and forth in front of your mouth. This is called a sound wave. When you speak into the Hearme Talkyou, it focuses the wiggle to make a surprisingly clear message over a long distance. How long can you make your Hearme Talkyou and still understand someone speaking into it?

TRY IT!

A Hearme Talkyou gets pretty good reception, but what if it were longer? What would happen if you added a third funnel midway on your tube? What do you hear if you put both funnels over your ears?

ITTY-BITTY SQUEAKADOOS

The Squeakadoos make music that's out of this world. As in, none of us know exactly where they came from. Maybe they're from your world, human friend? Regardless, they do have the voices of angels. Very high-pitched angels, but talented ones.

FAST FACTS

WHAT: Small, craft-stick critters that squeak with your breath
STEAM STUFF: sound and pitch ▪ **DIFFICULTY:** ★ ★ ▪ **COST:** $

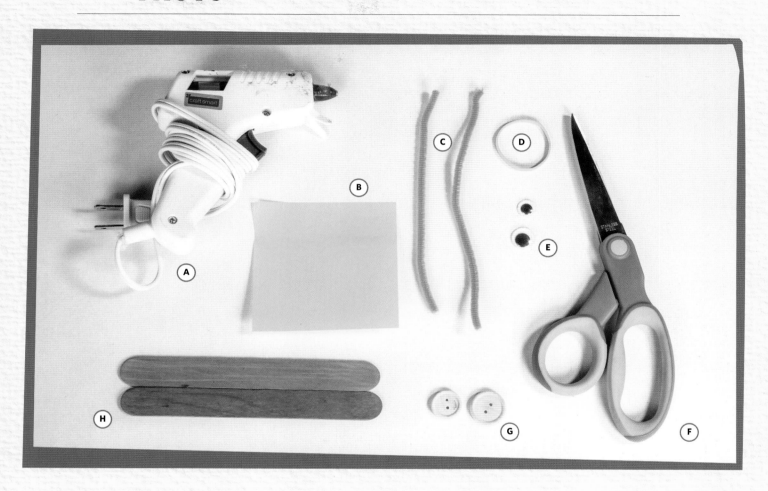

YOU WILL NEED

Ⓐ Glue gun Ⓑ 1 sticky note Ⓒ 2 pipe cleaners Ⓓ 1 rubber band Ⓔ Googly eyes Ⓕ Scissors
Ⓖ Buttons Ⓗ 2 jumbo craft sticks

MAKE YOUR CREATURE

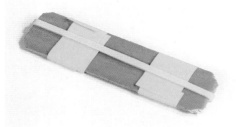

1. CUT OFF ROUND ENDS OF CRAFT STICKS. Save the rounded ends for later.

2. CUT AND WRAP 2 STICKY-NOTE STRIPS AROUND CRAFT STICK. Make sure each of the strips has a sticky part to it. Wrap the strips around and stick each to itself but not to the craft stick. This makes them slideable.

3. STRETCH RUBBER BAND AROUND 1 CRAFT STICK. Choose a rubber band that's taut, but not too tight, when stretched the long way across the craft stick.

4. TWIST PIPE CLEANERS TO SANDWICH 2 CRAFT STICKS TOGETHER. ◎ Make sure the 2 craft sticks are snug, but not too tight. You can adjust this later.

5. FLIP OVER AND ADD EYES. Make sure to glue the eyes to the craft stick that doesn't have the rubber band around it. Make a fun alien face!

6. GIVE 'EM A SQUEAK! Blow through the middle of the 2 craft sticks and let that squeak ring out. If it doesn't play right away, try adjusting the rubber band and pipe cleaners. What tune can you squeak out?

STEAM STUFF

How High Can a Squeak Get?

Squeakadoos have range. After all, most instruments can play different notes. A piano has different keys, a guitar has different strings and frets, and a Squeakadoo has its sticky-note strips. When you slide the strips closer together or farther apart, what happens to its squeak? When the strips are closer, there's less of the rubber band that can wobble back and forth. When they're pulled apart, there's more. This is just like putting your finger on different parts of a guitar string to make different the vibrating part longer or shorter. So what makes the highest squeak?

EXPLORE SOME MORE

Every Squeakadoo has its own voice. Depending on how tight the rubber band is, how long the craft stick is, and how close together the sticky-note strips are, it can make a higher or lower sound. Try making other Squeakadoos while changing these features, and you can get a whole musical range.

HONKSEE THE POPSTAR

OMG, did Honksee just look at us? *Aaaaaaaaaaaaa!* Okay, breathe, breathe, breathe. Sorry, human friend, it's just that Honksee is our favorite superstar in the entire Creature Kingdom. We've loved Honksee ever since her first album 327 years ago. And the last show we were at, Honksee honked right at us through the crowd. Even if Honksee won't sing with our band, let's go get an autograph.

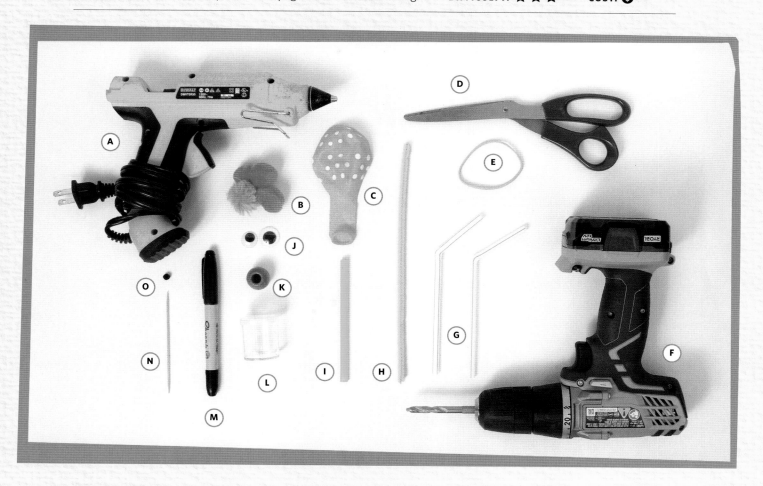

FAST FACTS

WHAT: Half popstar, half trombone that honks an adjustable note when you blow into the straw
STEAM STUFF: sound and pitch ▪ **DRILL TIME:** You'll need an adult helper with a drill to make this superstar. See page 10 for more on drilling. ▪ **DIFFICULTY:** ★★★ ▪ **COST:** $

YOU WILL NEED

Ⓐ Glue gun   Ⓑ A few large pompoms   Ⓒ 1 balloon   Ⓓ Scissors   Ⓔ 1 rubber band   Ⓕ Drill, with multiple bits

Ⓖ 2 bendy straws (either wider or thinner than straight straw)   Ⓗ 1 pipe cleaner   Ⓘ 1 straight straw   Ⓙ 2 googly eyes

Ⓚ 1 wooden bead   Ⓛ 1 very small plastic container   Ⓜ Marker   Ⓝ 1 toothpick   Ⓞ 1 tiny pompom

MAKE YOUR CREATURE

1. **DRILL 2 HOLES IN CONTAINER: ONE ON BOTTOM AND ONE IN SIDE.** ⊙ Carefully drill a hole in the bottom big enough for the straight straw, and drill another hole in the side for a bendy straw. The straws should fit snugly in the holes.

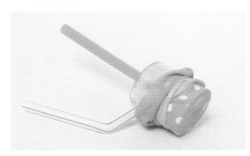

4. **STRETCH BALLOON OVER CONTAINER OPENING.** Make it tight like a drumhead, and use a rubber band to secure it.

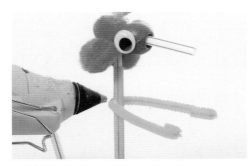

6. **GIVE HONKSEE SOME CHARACTER!** Honksee's got more personality than 5 creatures combined, so glue pompoms and googly eyes to the bendy straw to make a face. For arms, glue a bent pipe cleaner around the straight straw.

2. **PLACE STRAWS.** Fit the straight straw through the hole on bottom (no glue), and glue a bendy straw in the container's side hole.

5. **SLIDE OTHER BENDY STRAW INTO OR ONTO STRAIGHT STRAW.** The straw should fit loosely enough so that you can pull it up and down. This not only is Honksee's head, but also makes it so you can play multiple notes.

7. **MAKE HONKSEE A MICROPHONE.** Draw on a toothpick with a black marker. Next, glue on a tiny pompom, cut the toothpick short, and Honksee's got a mic!

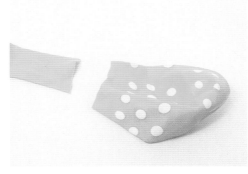

3. **CUT OFF BALLOON NECK.** You only need the rounded top part of the balloon.

8. **GIVE THAT POPSTAR A STAGE!** Adjust the straight straw so it's pushing against the tight balloon. Blow into Honksee's tail, and keep adjusting the straight straw until you hear a beautiful honk!

STEAM STUFF
SOUND AND PITCH

Honksee rose to galactic fame with a little help from science. When you blow into Honksee's tail, it plays a sound. But how? Try tracing the path the air takes through Honksee for a clue. When you blow into the straw, your breath adds pressure to the plastic container. The balloon expands and lets a little bit of air out of the straight straw before closing again. It does this over and over very quickly, causing vibration. That's where the sound comes from! Try touching the balloon with your hands while you play. You may also notice that by adjusting Honksee's neck, you can make the sound higher or lower, otherwise known as adjusting the *pitch* of the sound. How can you make a low note? What about a high note? Find out what changes the pitch with other musical instruments. Look around and keep your ears open!

TRY IT!

Try playing a note while adjusting the length of Honksee's neck. What happens to the note? What if you change the position of the straight straw against the balloon? How many different sounds can you play?

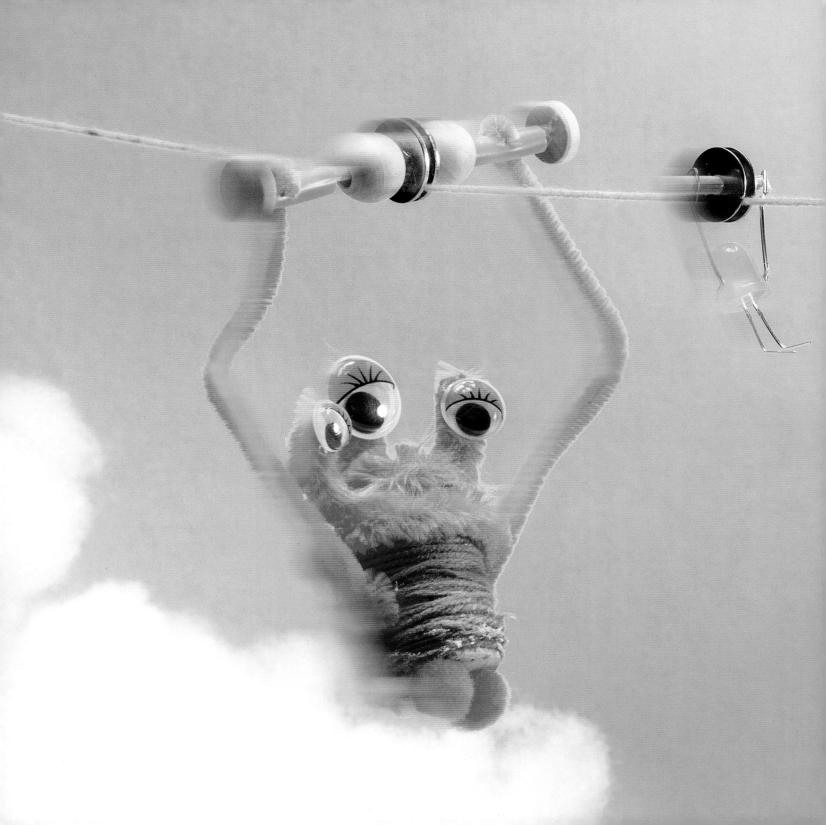

4
UPAND TOWN

IS IT HOT UP HERE OR AM I JUST SCARED?

We're not really afraid of heights, just terrified of falling. You'd catch us, though, right? With you around, Upand Town is a great place to be. Everything around here flies, jumps, and zips! You'll see the **Springy Launchums** (page 76) mid-blastoff, the **Bubbly Bubbloons** (page 80) floating about, the **Sticky-Footed Jumpees** (page 84) performing acrobatics, and the **Zippin' Zozot** (page 88) right here scootching along with us. Oh, can you hear that countdown? Let's zip down to see the Launchums before they take off!

SPRINGY LAUNCHUMS

Three! Two! One! *WHOOSH!* I know what you're thinking:
a real-life superhero! Springy is pretty famous now, but
Reddi and I went to school with her when she was just
a student at Creature High School. You'd see her one second,
and then *BOOM!* she blasts off to who-knows-where.
Some creatures need their space, but she needs
outer space.

WHAT: A high-flying superhero launched by a spring ▪ **STEAM STUFF:** potential energy
DRILL TIME: You'll need an adult helper with a drill to make your launchpad. See page 10 for more on drilling. ▪ **DIFFICULTY:** ★ ▪ **COST:** $

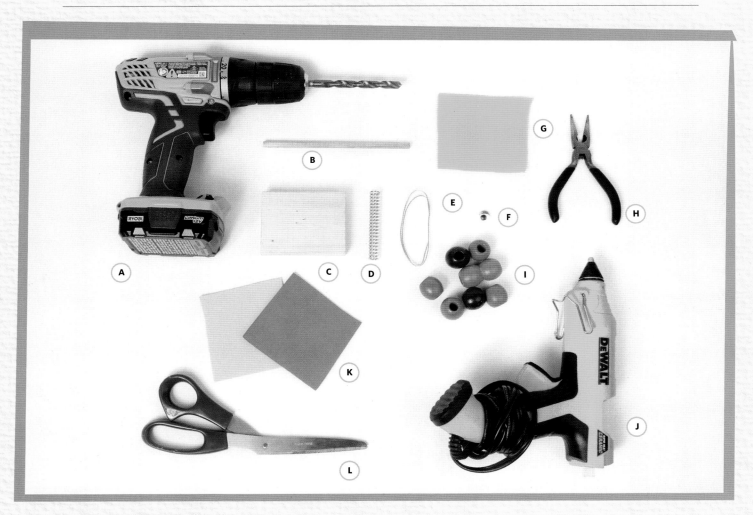

YOU WILL NEED

(A) Drill (with bit same size as dowel)   (B) 1 dowel (smaller than spring)   (C) 1 small wood block

(D) 1 spring (big enough to fit loosely around dowel)   (E) Posable steel wire   (F) Googly eyes   (G) Scrap of felt

(H) Pliers   (I) 2 wood beads (that can fit on dowel)   (J) Glue gun   (K) Scraps of craft foam, paint, and/or markers

(L) Scissors

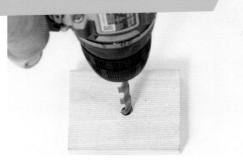

1. **DRILL HOLE IN WOOD BLOCK.** Choose a drill bit the same width as your dowel. Make a hole that goes directly down and halfway through your wood block.

2. **FIT IN DOWEL AND SPRING.** Make sure the dowel fits in the hole and that the spring fits loosely around the dowel.

3. **DECORATE THE LAUNCHER.** Launch with some flair! Use foam, paint, or pens to give your launcher some life.

4. **MAKE WIRE ARMS.** With the pliers, bend the wire to make posable arms and hands.

5. **USE BEADS AND WIRE TO MAKE BODY.** Glue together 2 beads so their holes line up, and glue the arms around the seam between them.

6. **GIVE SPRINGY A FACE.** Every superhero needs an identity, secret or not. Add a felt cape, googly eyes, and a face that expresses your Springy Launchum's personality.

7. **BLAST OFF!** Put your Launchum on the dowel, pull it down to squeeze the spring, and release it to send it skyward!

STEAM STUFF
POTENTIAL ENERGY

Some things just love bouncing back: rubber bands, rubber balls, and even springs. So what gives that spring its springiness? The energy that launches your Launchum has to come from somewhere. When you pull down the spring with your Launchum on it, you are putting in the energy that the spring is going to use moments later to blast off. By squishing the spring, you are giving it *potential energy*, which means energy that can be used at a later time. When you let go, the spring wants to be back in its original shape, and in doing so launches your superhero. Try looking for other things in the world that bounce back. After all, they're the things with lots of potential.

TRY IT!

No two Launchums fly alike. How high can you make a Launchum fly? What about how far? What if you used only one bead or changed the angle of your launcher? What about changing the design of your superhero monster?

BUBBLY BUBBLOONS

Wow, look at that bubble! And that one and that one and that one and that one and that one! Look at that cube-shaped bubble. Ooh, and that triangle one. Most of the bubbles in your world are round, right, human friend? Here in Upand Town, the Bubbloons make bubbles into all sorts of shapes with their bodies. Let's float on over and check them out.

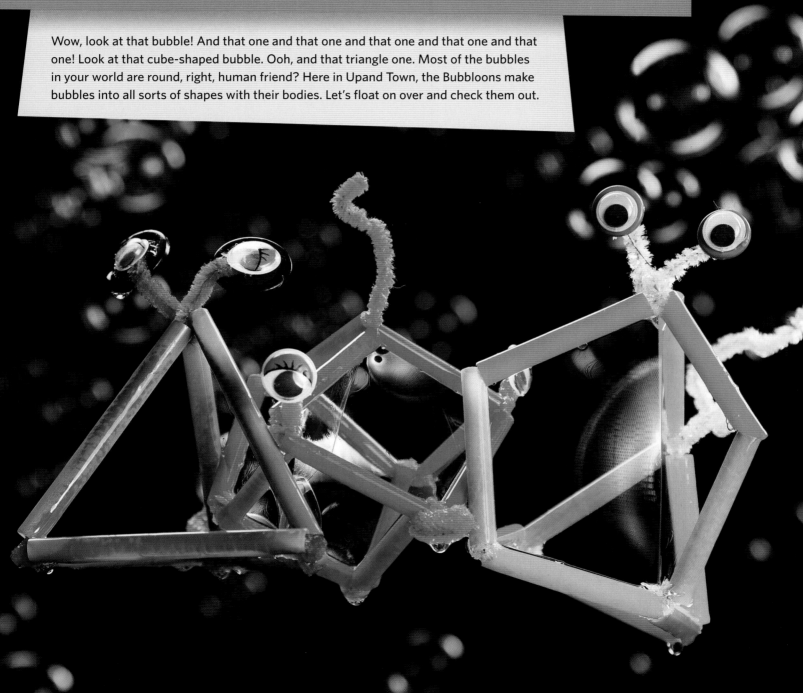

WHAT: 3-dimensional straw shapes that make amazing geometry when dipped in bubble solution
STEAM STUFF: geometry ▪ **DIFFICULTY:** ★ ▪ **COST:** $

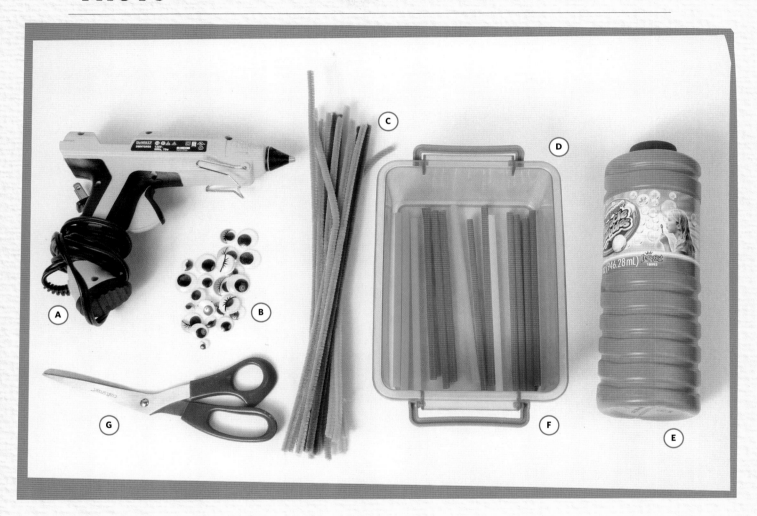

YOU WILL NEED

Ⓐ Glue gun   Ⓑ Several googly eyes   Ⓒ A bunch of pipe cleaners   Ⓓ A bunch of straws   Ⓔ Bubble solution (store-bought or homemade)   Ⓕ Container for bubble solution (a deep one works best)   Ⓖ Scissors

1. **CUT STRAWS INTO PIECES OF EQUAL LENGTH.** Start with around 12 pieces. You can always make more later.

2. **RUN A PIPE CLEANER THROUGH STRAWS TO CONNECT THEM AND MAKE A SHAPE.** Try starting off by making a square using 4 straw pieces. Twist the ends of the pipe cleaner together to secure the shape.

3. **REPEAT TO MAKE A FEW SIMILAR FLAT SHAPES.** Try starting with 3 or 4 squares just to get the hang of it.

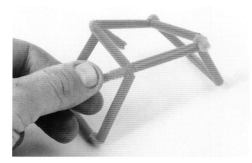

4. **CONNECT FLAT SHAPES WITH PIPE CLEANERS AND STRAWS TO MAKE A 3D SHAPE.** Connect your flat shapes with more pipe cleaners and extra straws (if needed).

5. **USE EXTRA PIPE CLEANER BITS TO MAKE ANTENNAE AND A TAIL.** A tail is super useful for dipping a Bubbloon in bubble solution, and antennae are great for gluing eyes onto. You can cut off the extra pipe cleaner you don't need.

6. **MAKE A FUN FACE.** Bubbloons aren't defined by their shape, but by their personality. Give yours some flair with googly eyes!

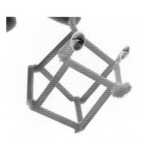

7. **IT'S BUBBLE TIME!** Pour bubble solution into a container deep enough so you can dip your Bubbloon all the way into the solution. What do you see when you pull out your Bubbloon? See how the shapes change over time. And of course, don't forget to blow some bubbles.

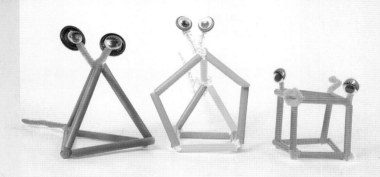

STEAM STUFF

GEOMETRY

You may have chosen your Bubbloon's shape, but what about the shapes within the shape? When you blow bubbles, they come out as little spheres, but what about the shapes of the soap film inside your Bubbloons? Can you figure out how to make the soap film form a triangle? Or even a little cube? Try holding your Bubbloon by the tail and dipping it all the way into the solution. What happens when you pull it out? What happens with a different-shaped Bubbloon? Some of the shapes formed inside are called *natural geometries*, and you find them in nature over and over again. They can be in anything from the shapes of crystals to the forms of honeybee homes. They just keep coming up! Which ones can you make?

EXPLORE SOME MORE

There are so many shapes to make! After you've made your first Bubbloon, try making some more. You can try a different number of straws, different lengths of straw, or arranging the straws differently. For a first step, try making a bunch of triangles and connecting them to make a larger shape.

STICKY-FOOTED JUMPEES

Shhhhh! Quiet on the course. Sorry, human friend, but the Jumpee is attempting its hardest trick yet. Out of the slingshot, into a high jump, and then into the very tiny (even for us) pool. No creature has done this since the Creature Olympics of 2936. Okay, grab hold of this rope. Here's the pullback, the release, aaaaaand . . .

FAST FACTS

WHAT: Slingshot-launched pompom creatures with magnetic feet ▪ **STEAM STUFF:** elastics

DRILL TIME: You'll need an adult helper with a drill to make your Jumpee. See page 10 for more on drilling.

READY, AIM, HOLD ON: Remember to aim at the targets, not your friends. ▪ **DIFFICULTY:** ★ ★ ▪ **COST:** $

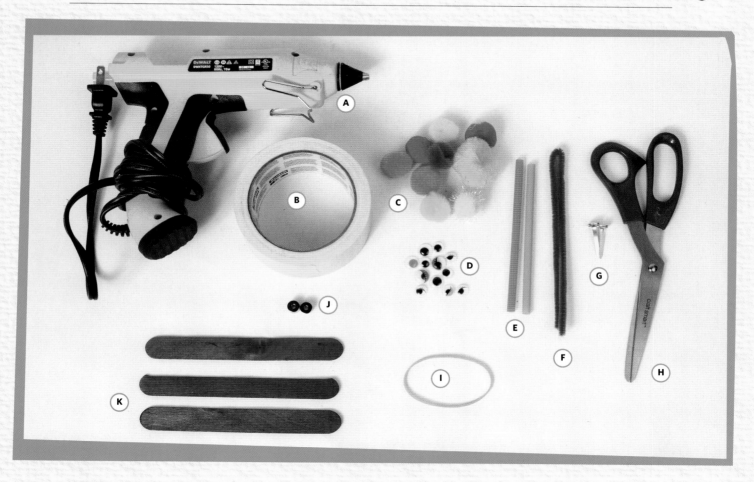

YOU WILL NEED

(A) Glue gun (B) Duct tape (C) Pompoms (D) A few googly eyes (E) A few straws (F) Pipe cleaner (G) 2 metal brad fasteners (H) Scissors (I) 1 rubber band (J) 1 very small magnet (K) 3 large craft sticks ● Drill, with small bit

1. DRILL A HOLE THROUGH 2 OF THE CRAFT STICKS. Stack the sticks together and drill a small hole through 1 end of both sticks.

2. GLUE THE 3 CRAFT STICKS TOGETHER. Make the shape of an upside-down capital A. Use a good amount of hot glue to keep the shape secure during launch.

3. ATTACH RUBBER BAND WITH BRADS. Put a brad through each of the 2 drilled holes, and link them with a rubber band. Fold out the brads' legs to keep the rubber band secure.

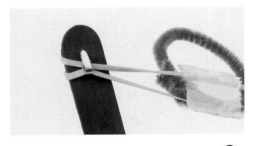

4. MAKE A JUMPEE HOLDER FOR LAUNCHER. ◎ Make a small loop with a pipe cleaner. Wrap a piece of duct tape around the rubber band and the pipe cleaner loop to make a pocket for your Jumpee and a handle to pull it back.

5. GLUE SMALL MAGNET ONTO A POMPOM. Jumpees are pompom creatures, and the magnets will make it so your Jumpee can stick to things when launched.

6. CUT 1 TO 3 DECORATIVE STRAW PIECES FOR ANTENNAE AND LEGS. Snip off small pieces of straw, and then make small cuts on 1 end of each straw and flare the ends. Glue them on to add pizazz, making sure not to cover up the magnet.

7. GIVE JUMPEE SOME STYLE. Besides the straws, add eyes, and any other decorations else you wish.

8. LAUNCH YOUR JUMPEE AND STICK THE LANDING! Place the Jumpee in the slingshot pocket, and pull it back. Make sure you are not aiming at people, pets, or breakable things. Let your Jumpee fly! If you aim at it at something made of steel, the magnet will stick to it!

STEAM STUFF

ELASTICS

It doesn't take much to launch a Jumpee. Pull back on that rubber band, and let it go to send your Jumpee flying. Rubber bands are pretty neat that way, and are a great example of an *elastic* material. That means it can stretch, and then it tries to return to its original shape. When you think about it, that's fairly unique. If you stretch out a ball of string, it doesn't leap back into a ball. Rubber bands do, and that's what makes them so great for launching things and so fun to play around with. What other elastic things can you find around your home?

TRY IT!

There isn't just one way to make a Jumpee slingshot. By adding rubber bands, changing the size of the launching pocket, and the shape of the crafts, you can actually get your Jumpee to go much, much higher or farther. What designs can you come up with to compare to your first launcher? What did you change?

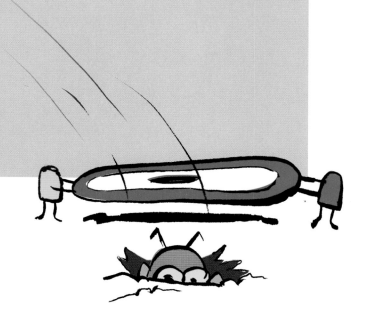

ZIPPIN' ZOZOTS

Wow, look at that Zozot zip on by! In fact, I don't think I've ever seen a Zozot that doesn't zip. They just seem to be having the best time all the time. Let's go join for the ride!

FAST FACTS

WHAT: A zip-lining creature that rides down a string! ■ **STEAM STUFF:** center of mass

ZIP-LINING: To send your Zozot zipping, find a large space where you can tape or tie up string for the Zozot to ride down ■ **DIFFICULTY:** ★ ★ ★ ■ **COST:** $

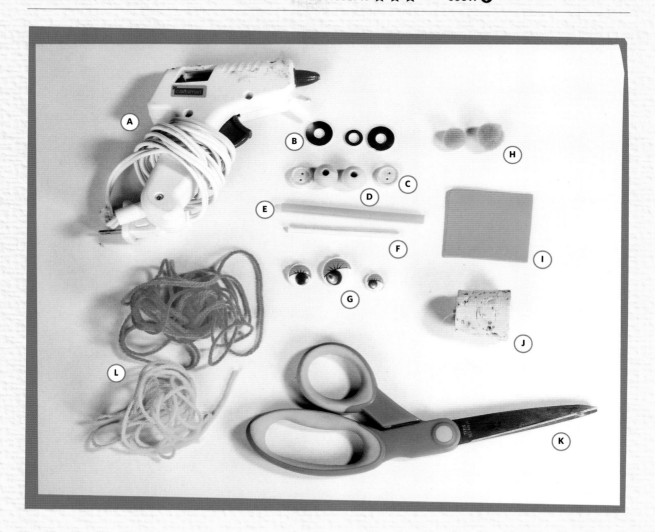

YOU WILL NEED

(A) Glue gun (B) 3 washers (2 large, 1 small) (C) 2 buttons (D) 2 beads (E) 1 straw (F) 1 skinny wood dowel (about 4 inches long) (G) Googly eyes (H) Pom-poms (I) Small scrap of craft foam (J) 1 cork (K) Scissors (L) Yarn ● 3 pipe cleaners (not pictured)

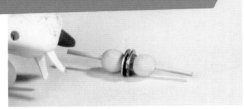

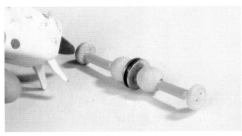

1. **GLUE WASHERS AND BEADS ON DOWEL.** Glue them snugly together like a sandwich. The beads are the bread, the big washers are next, and the small washer is in the middle.

2. **SLIDE ON STRAW PIECES AND GLUE BUTTONS.** Cut 2 straw pieces and slide them on either side of the beads. Glue buttons on the ends of the dowel to keep your straws on.

3. **DRESS YOUR ZOZOT.** Zozots come in many styles. Add some color to the cork to give it some flavor.

4. **GLUE ON PIPE CLEANER ARMS.** Cut 2 equal-size arms long enough to reach up above your Zozot's head, and glue them on to its body.

5. **ADD SOME FEET.** Sure, a Zozot mostly glides— but you can glue on some feet to complete its look.

6. **WRAP ZOZOT HANDS AROUND STRAWS.** ◎ To glide, your Zozot has to be holding the straw only. When you put it on the string, you'll need to make sure the string is in a loop made by its arms and the washer wheels.

7. **SEND THAT ZOZOT ON A RIDE.** Tape up a piece of string, attach your Zozot arms around it, and send your Zozot gliding!

STEAM STUFF

WHAT'S SPINNING?

When you take your Zozot for a spin, which parts are actually spinning? Try looking up close as you move your Zozot along. Do the washers spin? The straws? The dowel? The Zozot? The free-moving straws allow your Zozot to keep it cool while the wheel above it spins like crazy. The dowel acts as an *axle*, just like you might find on a bus or a bike. An axle allows the wheels to turn, without having to spin the whole vehicle along with it. So, look closely at how your Zozot zips by.

EXPLORE SOME MORE

Is your Zozot having trouble riding? Try adjusting your Zozot by bending its arms a different way or by making longer ones. You can also add weight like some coins or some clay to the bottom of the Zozot to make it more stable, and ride faster. See what you can make zip.

5

LOST FILES OF MISTER E.

THESE CREATURES HAVE TO BE MADE UP, RIGHT?

I've been rooting around in Mister E.'s files in the library, and I found some pictures of creatures that I've never even heard of before. But then again, I guess we didn't think humans existed until recently, either. . . . Anyway, look! There are legends written here about a banished wrestler named **Sweatzo the Giant** (page 98), a strange money eater called the **Wallet Walladoo** (page 102), lost remains of an ancient desert creature called **Fossilized Beetlebops** (page 106), and the only-once-seen **Snowblowing Yetitat** (page 110) of the great north. And look at this file on the **Foldy Poppowtum** (page 94). I think the file is a monster itself. Let's go find these creatures!

FOLDY POPPOWTUMS

I'm getting a weird feeling about this. I don't think this is a normal pile of papers *about* creatures, human friend. I think this one *is* a creature! Whenever I try to close it up, it tries to bite me!

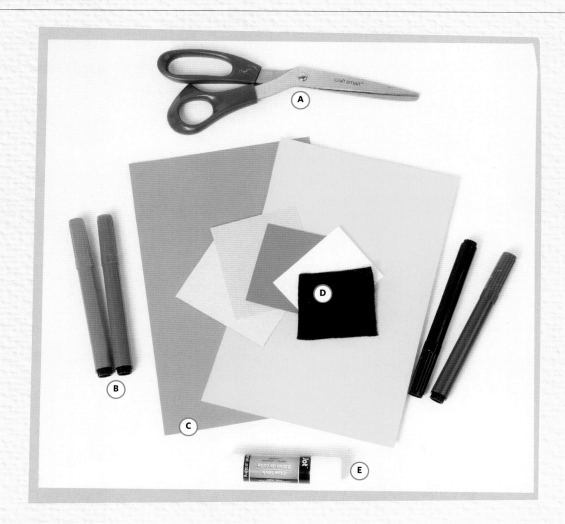

YOU WILL NEED

Ⓐ Scissors   Ⓑ Markers   Ⓒ 2 sheets cardstock (different colors)   Ⓓ Scraps of craft foam   Ⓔ Glue stick

MAKE YOUR CREATURE

1. **FOLD A SHEET OF CARDSTOCK IN HALF.**

2. **CUT SHORT SLIT IN THE MIDDLE.** Make the slit about 2 inches long, starting from the folded crease.

3. **FOLD AND CREASE TRIANGLES ON BOTH SIDES OF SLIT.** Fold your newly cut corners to make 2 triangles. Run your fingernails across the new folds to make a smooth crease. You can fold the triangles back and forth a few times to make the mouth work even better.

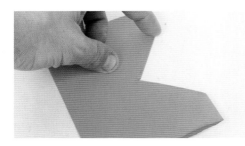

4. **TUCK TRIANGLES INSIDE FOLDED CARD.** ◎ Open the card just a tiny bit, and push the triangles to the inside so it looks like they're missing when you close the card again. This will make your Poppowtum's biting mouth.

5. **PUT A FACE ON IT!** Open up your card, and you should have a Poppowtum mouth pointing right at you. Draw and paste on eyes, teeth, nostrils, and a tongue. Try folding and unfolding the card a few times to see how the mouth and face change shape.

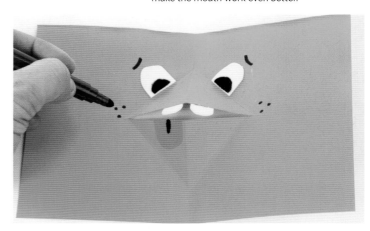

6. **CUT OUT POPPOWTUM.** Set your Poppowtum free! Cut out an outline in whatever creature form you wish. Your Poppowtum can have arms, legs, or even tentacles.

7. **FOLD THE SECOND PIECE OF CARDSTOCK IN HALF.** This will be the background card to which you will glue the Poppowtum.

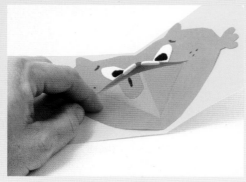

8. GLUE POPPOWTUM TO BACKGROUND CARDSTOCK. Using your glue stick, glue the creature so that the creases of the 2 sheets line up.

9. POP IT OUT! Try out your card! You can add more writing, add latches to keep the card closed, or even try mailing it to an unsuspecting person.

STEAM STUFF
STRUCTURE

Depending on how you fold flat materials, you can give them wildly different structures. These structures can be altered to make things compact, stronger, a special shape, or a special design. The Japanese practice of *origami* explores this idea. Engineers design ways to fold everything from a cardboard box for shipping to solar panels on a space shuttle. See what you can learn by changing the triangle folds of your creature's mouth. Once you start to experiment, you'll find fabulous things in the folds.

EXPLORE SOME MORE

That first cut means a lot. Depending on how long it is, what angle it makes, and where you cut that first slit in your cardstock, you can get completely different creature mouths. Try using other pieces of cardstock to make mouths and creatures of different shapes and sizes. See if you can figure out how to make the biggest bite!

SWEATZO THE GIANT

Legend says that Sweatzo sweats a lot under pressure. It seems like Sweatzo must always be under pressure, but don't let that stop you from getting into that ring. Just maybe bring an umbrella?

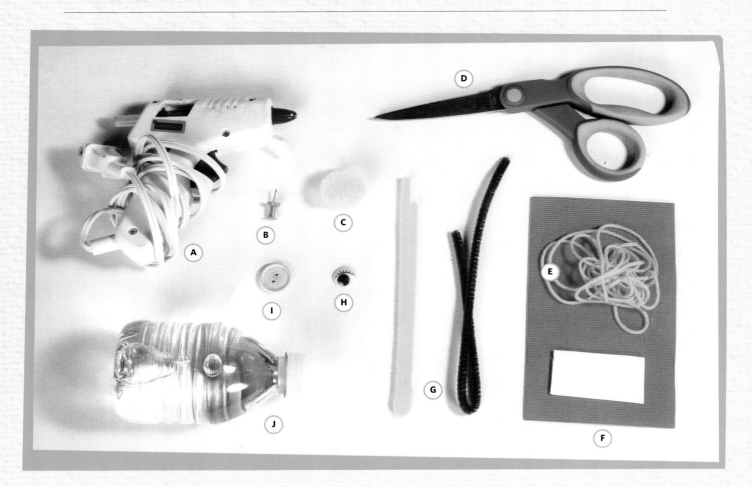

YOU WILL NEED

Ⓐ Glue gun   Ⓑ 1 pushpin   Ⓒ Pompoms   Ⓓ Scissors   Ⓔ Yarn   Ⓕ Craft foam pieces

Ⓖ 1 or 2 pipe cleaners   Ⓘ Googly eyes   Ⓙ Buttons   Ⓛ 1 small plastic bottle

MAKE YOUR CREATURE

1. **MAKE SWEATZO A HAT.** Glue some yarn and a pompom onto the bottle cap to begin Sweatzo's wardrobe.

2. **CUT OUT A COSTUME.** Is Sweatzo a wrestler? A swimmer? A world-class ice skater? Cut out a foam costume to dress Sweatzo for the event.

3. **GLUE ON ARMS AND EYE.** Cut your pipe cleaner in 2, and curl into 2 arms. Glue on the arms and an eye, so Sweatzo will be ready to go.

4. **POKE SMALL HOLES WITH PIN.** ◎ With a pushpin, poke a few holes below the water line in Sweatzo. (Fill and cap the bottle before beginning if it is not already full of water.) You might get a little wet here, but after you dry off, Sweatzo shouldn't leak. If Sweatzo is leaking, the holes might be too big.

5. **UNLEASH THE SWEAT.** Sweatzo's ready for the workout! Either squeeze Sweatzo or uncap it to turn it into a sweaty fountain. Or leave it as a prank for an unsuspecting water bottle thief.

STEAM STUFF

UNDER PRESSURE

Sweatzo is under a lot of pressure. You might think that when you poke a hole in the bottle, water would come flying out. But if the holes are tiny enough, Sweatzo doesn't sweat. The water inside actually sticks to itself and to the bottle, and it stays put. However, if you squeeze the bottle a little, it begins to sweat. Squeeze a little harder, and water comes flying out. Maybe even stranger is that if you uncap Sweatzo, water flies out too. It makes a great prank, but it also makes good science. Why do you think Sweatzo sweats when its hat is off?

TRY IT!

Not every pin prick is the same. The way Sweatzo sweats depends on how big you made the hole, and where the hole is placed. Try differently placed holes to see if you can find patterns with which ones squirt the farthest.

WALLET WALLADOO

The stories say that Walladoos love to eat money. Coins, bills, everything disappear into its giant mouth. They tried to tape its mouth shut, but tape seems to only make it stronger. We've never seen one until now, human friend, but I wouldn't get too close without feeding it. Got any spare change?

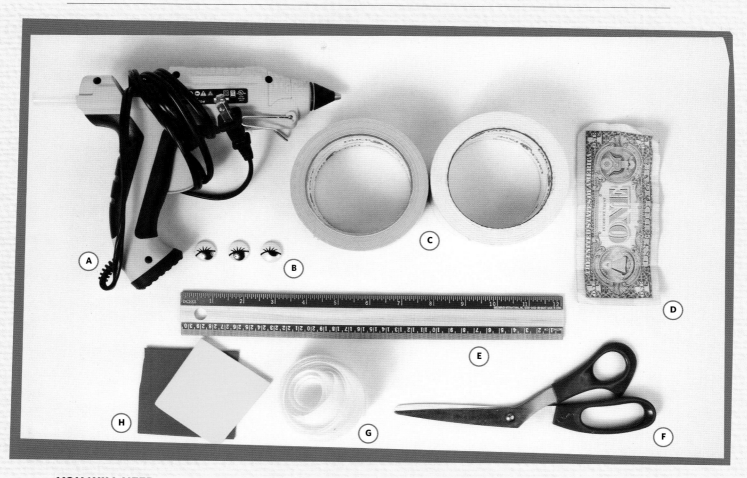

YOU WILL NEED

Ⓐ Glue gun   Ⓑ 3 large googly eyes   Ⓒ 2 rolls duct tape (different colors)   Ⓓ 1 dollar bill (for measurement)

Ⓔ Ruler   Ⓕ Scissors   Ⓗ Small pieces of craft foam   Ⓖ 8 inches Velcro (both sides)

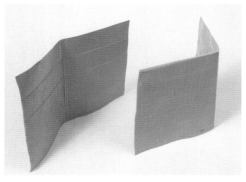

1. **MAKE A DUCT TAPE MAT.** Lay down 3 8-inch strips of duct tape, sticky side up, so they overlap slightly. Repeat, and sandwich the 2 duct tape mats together, sticky sides in.

2. **TRIM DUCT TAPE EDGES TO MAKE A RECTANGLE.** Make sure the remaining duct tape mat is still larger than a dollar bill.

3. **REPEAT STEPS 1 AND 2 TO MAKE A MATCHING DUCT TAPE MAT.**

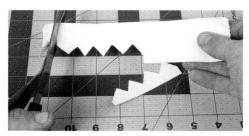

4. **TAPE THE 2 SHORT SIDES AND 1 LONG SIDE OF THE 2 MATS TOGETHER.** Fold a piece of duct tape over the 3 seams, and trim off the edges for a neat, clean look.

5. **CUT TEETH OUT OF A DUCT TAPE MAT.** Using your other roll of duct tape, tape 2 strips together, sticky sides in. Cut out 2 rows of teeth the same length as the short sides of your wallet.

6. **MAKE A FOAM TONGUE, AND GLUE.** Cut out a tongue from craft foam. Glue it and the teeth to the short sides of the wallet.

7. **GLUE DOWN VELCRO STRIPS.** On the side with the tongue, glue down 2 strips of fuzzy Velcro. On the other side, glue a long strip of the Velcro's prickly side. When you fold the mouth in half, the prickly strip and fuzzy strips should stick together.

8. **MAKE A FACE.** Glue on some googly eyes, and make eyebrows out of craft foam. Give your Walladoo any character you want!

9. **PUT YOUR MONEY WHERE WALLADOO'S MOUTH IS!** Feed Walladoo some cash, and carry it around! Go on the town, and see what kind of reactions you get to your monstrous money keeper.

EXPLORE SOME MORE

Customize your Walladoo to make it uniquely yours. You can add all sorts of pockets and designs on the inside! Start by adding some pockets that can hold coins or cards. To make them, sandwich strips of duct tape together, sticky-sides in, to make mats. Then trim their edges to fit. You can use other strips of duct tape or hot glue to attach your new pockets inside your Walladoo.

FOSSILIZED BEETLEBOPS

Okay, the map said turn left at the Walladoo and to start digging right at this X. I don't see an X on the ground, but let's start anyway. The papers said we might find a fossil of a creature that hasn't existed for a kajillion years. But if nobody's found it yet, what are the chances that we would find anyth—wait! My shovel just hit something!

FAST FACTS

WHAT: A plaster cast made in clay that reveals an old buggy fossil ▪ **STEAM STUFF:** chemistry, earth science ▪ **ROCK OUT:** This activity requires some waiting time! Normally it takes Earth thousands of years to make fossils, but your fossil will harden in 45 to 60 minutes. ▪ **DIFFICULTY:** ★ ★ ▪ **COST:** $ $

YOU WILL NEED

(A) Food coloring (optional) (B) A little water (C) Small blob of clay (D) A couple of scoops of Plaster of Paris (or cement) (E) 1 plastic spoon (F) 1 mixing stick (G) Assortment of small objects (to press into clay) (H) 1 large wooden bead or small ball ● 2 small paper cups

1. **PRESS CLAY IN BOTTOM OF PAPER CUP.** Make it about 1 inch thick. Use your thumb to smooth out the surface of the clay.

2. **PRESS A LARGE BEAD INTO CLAY.** Make a rounded imprint in your clay to make your Beetlebop's body. Remove the bead carefully to leave its imprint intact.

3. **MAKE MORE BEETLEBOP FEATURES BY PRESSING IN OTHER OBJECTS.** Toothpicks, beads, zip ties, and pencils are all great for adding buggy details such as antennae, eyes, or legs. Press the items in and pull them out, leaving their impressions behind.

OPTIONAL

4. **MIX WATER WITH PLASTER OF PARIS.** ◉ In a separate cup, mix approximately equal parts water and plaster, so that your result has the consistency of toothpaste. Too runny? Add plaster. Too stiff? Add water.

5. **STIR FOOD COLORING INTO THE MIX.** Add 3 or 4 drops of food coloring to the plaster mix to give your fossil some color.

6. **SLOWLY POUR PLASTER MIX INTO CLAY MOLD.** Cover the Beetlebop's imprint completely with plaster and pour a little extra on top.

7. **WAIT ABOUT 45 MINUTES.** Afterward, you can check how the fossil is doing by giving a tap on the sides and top. If the plaster is still a little mushy, wait a couple of minutes more. If it's solid, it's ready to go!

8. **EXCAVATE YOUR FOSSIL!** Peel away the cup, pull out the fossil, and give it a clean! It's ready for your home museum!

STEAM STUFF

MIXING ROCK

You may not know it, but you just rocked! When you added water to your plaster, you set a *chemical reaction* in motion. It's the same chemical reaction that is happening all around Earth, the one that makes new *sedimentary* rock. But how do animal shapes get in there and make fossils? It starts when an animal or plant dies in some muck. Minerals and water mix around it and cast it into the stone. This usually takes place over many years, and some fossils found on Earth are over a billion years old. As the rock forms, it gives off heat, which you can actually feel by holding your cup as its contents harden. Can you feel the heat? If so, that's a good sign that your reaction is underway. You have now joined an old tradition of mixing new rock.

TRY IT!

What would you look like in fossil form? For your next Beetlebop, use your thumb instead of a bead to make the body. Push your thumb slowly into the clay and remove it carefully. You'll be able to see your fingerprints in the rock!

SNOWBLOWING YETITAT

We're in search of the Yetitat, a creature that creates and blows all the snowstorms in the kingdom. We don't know where it is or even exactly *what* it is—oh, do you think it's that giant, scary-looking thing on that snow mound? That thing could make snowballs bigger than my face!

FAST FACTS

WHAT: A motorized, fan-blowing creature of the great north ▪ **STEAM STUFF:** airflow, electronics
MAKING CIRCUITS: This project requires a DC motor, which may need to be ordered online in advance. ▪ **DIFFICULTY:** ★ ★ ★ ▪ **COST:** $ $

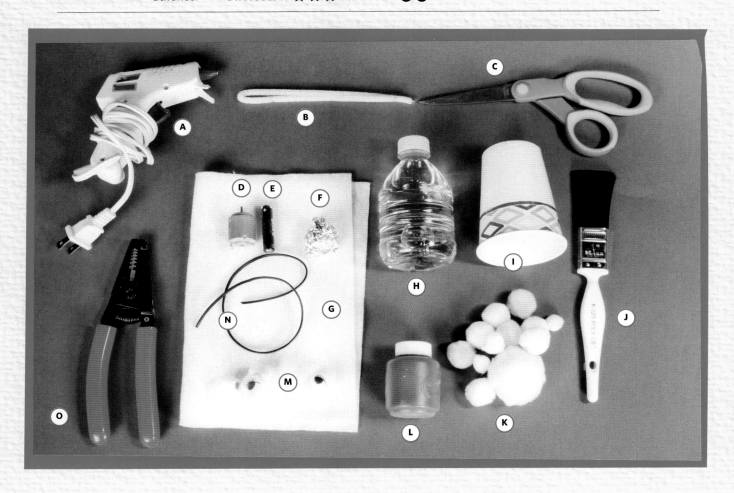

YOU WILL NEED

Ⓐ Glue gun   Ⓑ 2 pipe cleaners   Ⓒ Scissors   Ⓓ 11.5-3V DC motor   Ⓔ 1 AAA battery   Ⓕ Small ball of tin foil

Ⓖ 1 piece of felt big enough to cover the cup   Ⓗ 1 small plastic bottle   Ⓘ 1 cup   Ⓙ/Ⓛ Paint and brush (optional)

Ⓚ Pompoms   Ⓜ Googly eyes   Ⓝ 2 6-inch wires (or 1 2-stranded wire)   Ⓞ Wire strippers   ● Tape

1. **WRAP CUP IN FELT.** Cut the felt to size, wrap it around the cup, and finish with a line of hot glue.

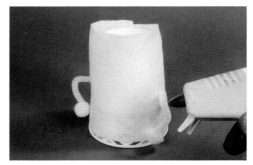

2. **ATTACH PIPE CLEANER ARMS.** Glue pompoms and pipe cleaners to the Yetitat's sides.

3. **MAKE A POMPOM-FULL FACE.** Place pompoms under the eyes and the head for a fluffy crown effect.

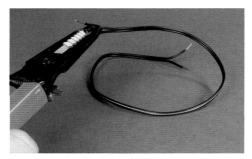

4. **STRIP WIRE ENDS.** Use your wire strippers to expose ½ inch of wire on each of the 4 ends.

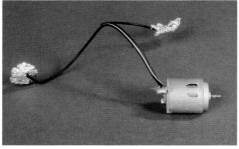

5. **ATTACH 1 END OF EACH WIRE TO MOTOR AND OTHER TO TIN FOIL.** Bend 2 of the wire ends around the motor tabs, and crumple foil balls around the other 2 ends.

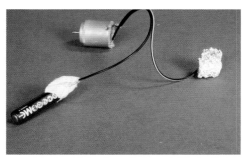

6. **TAPE 1 TIN FOIL BALL TO TOP OF BATTERY.**

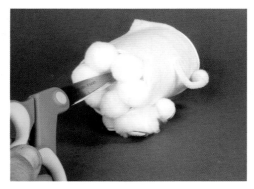

7. **MAKE HOLE IN TOP OF CUP.** This should be large enough to fit your motor through.

8. **GLUE MOTOR IN AMONG POMPOMS.** Make sure the end is sticking up and out of the pompoms.

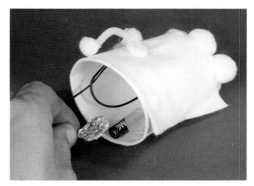

9. **TAPE BATTERY INSIDE CUP.** Make sure in it's a position easy for you to access with the 1 free wire.

10. CUT TOP OFF PLASTIC BOTTLE. Keep the cap and the rounded part of the bottle.

11. CUT AND FOLD FAN BLADES OUT OF PLASTIC BOTTLE. ◎ Cut vertical strips, and then bend each of the strips sideways the same way to make a flower-like ring.

12. PAINT FAN. Add some color to that Yetitat head.

13. MAKE HOLE IN CAP AND PUSH CAP ON TO MOTOR. Use scissors to make a hole in the bottle cap, and glue it on to the end of the motor.

14. BLOW A WINDSTORM! Press the free foil ball on the other end of the battery to start the fan. Why try to predict the weather when you can make your own?

STEAM STUFF
NUMBER ONE FAN

If you're a fan of fans, you'll start to see them everywhere: in homes, in buildings, on airplanes, even inside computers. Each one is made of *blades*, which are the long things that spin around. When the blades spin, they each push air, sending it off one way or the other. Depending on their shape, size, and position, they can make quite a gust. Try playing around with the Yetitat's head fan to see if you can create a storm.

TRY IT!

Try bending the fan blades into another formation. How does it change the way your Yetitat blows air? How can you make it blow outward, upward, or downward? What about harder and softer? What happens when they're not all bent the same way?

FINAL WORDS FROM REDDI & YULLO

Oh my, human friend, what a wonderful adventure.

Look at all those creatures you made along the way!

We'll miss you in this world, but I'm sure
yours needs you too.

And of every creature here, you'll always be
the most curious of them all.

INDEX

ACKNOWLEDGMENTS

These creatures would still just be piles of straws and craft sticks if it weren't for the following helpful humans. Thank you to all of them for lending their wild talents and imaginations.

Dayoung Cho, supernatural designer, who could make even a jar of cat toenails look like the cutest thing you've ever seen in your whole life. Thank you for making these creatures look their sharpest.

Jeffrey Schwinghammer, omnipotent photographer, for playing wizard with lights and camera to open up a portal from our world to the creatures'. Thank you for making these projects sparkle.

Trevor Spencer, master illustrator, for being able to wave his magic wand of a pen at a bunch of plastic straws and craft sticks and turn them into imaginative drawings on the page. Thank you for giving life to these humble creations.

Also a big thank you to the following folks, who helped in ways bigger than they knew. **Hannah Shulman,** infinitely patient enabler of crafting mayhem. **Thom O'Hearn,** best book coach in the biz. **Arvind Gupta,** inspiring friend and broadcaster of so many good things. **The Exploratorium**, provider of creative space and factory of wonderful ideas. **Dan Sudran** and the **Mission Science Workshop**, for giving me the place to learn as I taught.

ABOUT THE AUTHOR

Sam Haynor loves things that go *whoosh*, *ping*, *doink*, and *bonk*! Sam has below-average crafting skills but an above-average love of pompoms. He graduated from some places and worked at others, and has been greatly inspired by his students and their incredible imaginations that never seem to stop inventing. While teaching, he became hooked on the idea that change in one's life can come from making things that are personally meaningful—or even making things from trash. He really likes trash. Come find him at the Exploratorium museum in San Francisco, where he currently works as an Exhibit Developer. He'll probably try to convince you to help him build something.